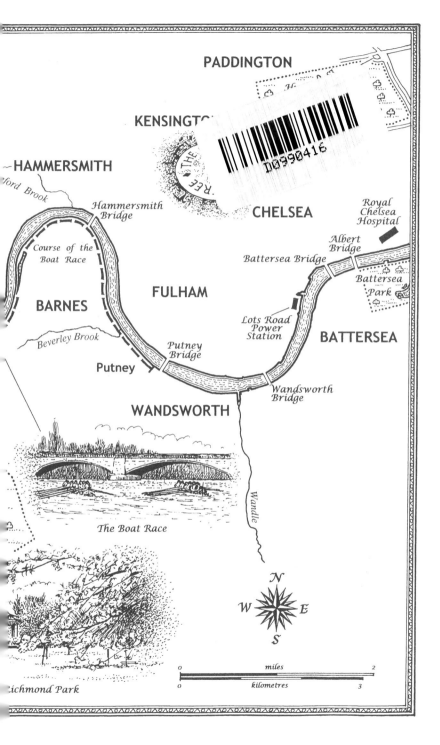

PADDINGTON

KENSINGTON

~HAMMERSMITH

*ford Brook*

*Hammersmith
Bridge*

CHELSEA

Royal
Chelsea
Hospital

*Course of the
Boat Race*

Albert
Bridge

*Battersea Bridge*

Battersea
Park

BARNES

FULHAM

*Beverley Brook*

*Lots Road
Power
Station*

BATTERSEA

*Putney
Bridge*

Putney

*Wandsworth
Bridge*

WANDSWORTH

*Wandle*

*The Boat Race*

N

W E

S

*Richmond Park*

| miles | | 2 |

0

| kilometres | | 3 |

0

# London's Thames

# London's Thames

GAVIN WEIGHTMAN

JOHN MURRAY

© Gavin Weightman 2004

First published in Great Britain in 2004 by John Murray (Publishers)
A division of Hodder Headline

The right of Gavin Weightman to be identified as the Author of the
Work has been asserted by him in accordance with the Copyright,
Designs and Patents Act 1988.

1 3 5 7 9 10 8 6 4 2

All rights reserved. No part of this publication may be reproduced,
stored in a retrieval system, or transmitted, in any form or by any means
without the prior written permission of the publisher, nor be otherwise
circulated in any form of binding or cover other than that in which it is
published and without a similar condition being imposed on the
subsequent purchaser.

A CIP catalogue record for this title is available from the British Library

ISBN 0-7195-6411 5

Typeset in 11/13pt Monotype Bembo by
Servis Filmsetting Ltd, Manchester

Printed and bound in Great Britain by
Clays Ltd, St Ives plc

Hodder Headline policy is to use papers that are natural, renewable and
recyclable products and made from wood grown in sustainable forests.
The logging and manufacturing processes are expected to conform to
the environmental regulations of the country of origin.

John Murray (Publishers)
338 Euston Road
London NW1 3BH

# Contents

## CONTENTS

# *Introduction*

There is no better place to contemplate the long and fascinating history of the River Thames than the centre of the slender Millennium footbridge, now that engineers have solved the problem of its unnerving vibrations. It spans the river between St Paul's Cathedral on the north bank and the Tate Modern art gallery directly across the water to the south. Face downstream, to the east, and the view is dominated by Tower Bridge which stands astride the river like a fairy castle. Beyond it, the Thames gradually widens on its sixty-mile course to the North Sea.

Look down through the slender silver wires of the Millennium Bridge and you might see that on the swirling brown surface of the river the flotsam and jetsam is racing westwards, towards Parliament, away from the sea. The Thames, it seems, is running backwards, flowing strongly 'upstream'. Later the river will turn, and the water level along the Embankment walls will begin to fall rapidly, revealing gravel beaches. At the turn of the tide, roughly every six hours, there are a few minutes of calm water, then the Thames is on the move again, rushing into London from the sea.

You will not see this flow of millions of gallons of water back and forth from any bridge in Paris, for the Seine is tidal only as far upstream as Rouen, and glides through the French capital in one direction only. One overwhelming historical fact about the River Thames, the significance of which is invariably overlooked by both visitors to London and Londoners themselves, is that it is tidal, all the way from its wide estuary to the lock at Teddington in Middlesex, on the western fringes of the capital.

This flow of water, running at a treacherous six or seven knots, packs enormous power which was harnessed for centuries to supply London with everything from food to building materials, right up to the age of electricity. It was the Thames tides which gave rise to the windowless monster of the Tate Modern art gallery, for it began life in 1947 as a power station, fuelled by coal shipped upriver from the north-east of England. On the north bank, St Paul's stands testimony to the power of the Thames tides. Most of the stone and timber used to build it between 1675 and 1710 came up the river, in the days when the roads in England were pot-holed tracks, when there were no canals to speak of and steam railways were a futuristic dream.

In his poem *The Waste Land* the American T.S. Eliot called the river 'a strong brown God'. If that was true of the Mississippi of his childhood in St Louis, it was even more so of the Thames, which Eliot knew well from the many years he spent in London. A sailing ship could weigh anchor near the mouth of the Thames as the flood tide began, and for six hours it would be carried inland, given a free ride on the river. Leaving the Pool of London – the reaches immediately below London Bridge – the same ship could get a free ride back to sea on the ebb tide.

Much can be learnt about the river from this one vantage point on the new Millennium Bridge. Take another look at Tower Bridge. When was it built? 1066? Unlikely, though its architecture appears to reflect the Tower of London which it overshadows. It is often said that the Americans who, in 1967, bought the early nineteenth-century London Bridge thought they were getting Tower Bridge which looks so much more 'historic'. Like all myths this has a point: very few landmarks instantly say London, and Tower Bridge is one of them. It is, however, little over a century old and has a steel frame structure: the stone fascia is just cladding.

Before leaving the Millennium Bridge, you might try baiting a hook with a worm and tossing your line into the river. It does not look promising, but the chances are that you will pull out a fish. Not a salmon perhaps, but certainly a silvery roach or one of the dozens of species that have returned to the river since the great clean-up in the 1960s. Faulty sewage works and bomb damage to pipes had killed nearly all life in the metropolitan reaches of the Thames by the 1950s. The first sign that the fish were coming back after a long period of refurbishment of the sewage system was the catch made by the filters of the coal-fired electricity power stations like the original Bankside, now the Tate Modern art gallery. History was repeating itself. The site on which Bankside was built had been a fish market in the fourteenth century.

Along the banks of the Thames is layer upon layer of London's past, much of it still visible, much of it long gone. This book aims to leave no important stone unturned as it surveys the river and its historical significance in the rise and growth of London, from the Woolwich Flood Barrier in the east to Kew Bridge and Richmond Park in the west.

Its scope is limited to those reaches of the river for purely practical reasons. To include the great sweep of the river as it widens into the estuary as well as the picturesque miles above Kew Bridge would make it much too long. The focus is on London and the hope is that, while it is written with the visitor in mind, it can be read with interest by those who have not yet seen Tower Bridge or the Houses of Parliament as well as by Londoners themselves. The profound influence exerted by the Thames on the rise and growth of London is a classic study of the immense, if often underrated, importance to a city's development of rivers which today might appear to be no more than inconsequential features of the urban landscape. If the 'creative' power of the Thames has waned, its destructive potential remains: it is still, as Eliot would have it, 'a strong brown God'.

# I

# London-on-sea

~

Moored just above Tower Bridge is the Royal Navy cruiser HMS *Belfast*, which has been a tourist attraction for the past thirty years. It is a sizeable ship, 11,000 tons, and a reminder of something which is not very evident today – London is, or was, a seaport. There was a time when this stretch of the river just below London Bridge was crammed with ocean-going vessels: such was the scene in Charles Dickens's day and it continued so long afterwards. One of the most vivid descriptions of the riverscape in the mid-nineteenth century is by that meticulous chronicler of London life, the journalist and contemporary of Dickens, Henry Mayhew:

> As I stood looking down upon the river the hundred clocks of the churches around me – with the golden figures on their black faces winking in the sunshine – chimed the hour of two in a hundred different tones, while solemnly, above all, boomed forth the monster bell of St Paul's, filling the air for minutes afterwards with a sweet melodious moan; and scarcely had it died away than there arose from the river the sharp tinkle of 'four bells' from the multitude of ships and steamers below. Indeed there was an exquisite charm in the different sounds that smote the ear from the busy Port of London. Now you would hear the tinkling of the distant purl-man's bell [a beer seller on the river] as in his boat he flitted in and out among the several tiers of colliers. Then

would come the rattle of some chain suddenly let go; after this, the chorus of many seamen heaving at the ropes, while, high above all, would be heard the hoarse voice of someone from the shore bawling through his hands to his mate aboard a ship in the river . . . As you looked down on the endless vista of masts that crowded each side of the river you could not help feeling how every power known to man was used to buy and diffuse the riches of every part of the world over this little island.

There are retired dockers in London who can still recall going up on to Tower Bridge in the morning in the hope of seeing a ship moored, unloading bacon from Denmark. For them it might have meant a day's work at one of the riverside wharves. But no sea shanties have been heard on the river for many years and the old sailor town along Ratcliff Highway has long since disappeared. London has the feel now of an inland town on a river, like Paris. But it is not: London is still 'on sea' and though the ocean-going merchant shipping has vanished, cruise liners now ride the tides up to Tower Bridge, where the passengers get a special thrill to see the bascules of London's Thames 'Gateway' open for them as they ease in to moor alongside HMS *Belfast*.

On their way upriver to Tower Bridge, the cruise ships pass through the glistening shields of the Thames Barrier at Woolwich, designed to shut out the sea when the tides rise dangerously high, then past the Greenwich Royal Observatory where the meridian line for the world's shipping was fixed in 1884, and on past what was once the vast dockland region now given over to new blocks of flats, offices and all kinds of watery recreation. But exciting as it is to see London from the Thames, very few foreign visitors arrive by ship as they once did.

However, if you fly over London and the weather is clear, you can in many ways get a better sense from a few thousand feet up of London's relation to the sea than you would on the river itself. The Thames Valley, in which London lies, spreads out below like a page from a school atlas. It is wide and shallow and the river

*A nostalgic reminder that London is on sea. In 1934, 1,500 tons of sand was spread on the foreshore by Tower Bridge to create an artificial beach for those who could not afford a holiday on the coast. The tides came and went just as they did at the seaside. This photograph is from 1952, before Tower Beach was closed for health reasons.*

estuary very long and narrow so that it appears to slice southern England halfway through from east to west. In fact the river was for much of its history a great natural frontier dividing the tribes of pre-Roman Britain. If you can pick out Tower Bridge – something the German Luftwaffe had no difficulty in doing even in their night-time bombing raids during the Second World War – you will see that the built-up area of the metropolis spreads around it in a great, rough-edged circle. Though London is a long way from the east coast, it became in the nineteenth century the greatest seaport in the world. For this, according to the most authoritative historians, Londoners can thank the Romans who, nearly two thousand years ago, were merely looking for the most advantageous place to build a bridge across the river.

# 2

# The first London

~

It is possible today to stand on the spot where London was founded. You will be surrounded by office blocks on a busy road, Lower Thames Street, in the City of London two hundred yards or so away from the northern end of London Bridge. Imagine the River Thames washing in on the flood tide and lapping at your feet. Looking back across the widening river you would see to the south a low-lying area with several gravel islands. Behind you on the north bank would be a low wooded hill. When it was founded, Londinium was no more than a Roman military encampment in a wild and sparsely inhabited river valley.

The Romans had no intention of founding a city here. Their only purpose was to establish a short cut from the Kent coast in the south, where they had made the Channel crossing from Gaul, to their garrison town of Colchester to the north-east. They were consolidating a foothold they had established on this far-flung outpost of their empire nearly a century earlier, when Julius Caesar landed on the Kent coast, near Deal, and marched north as a would-be conqueror. Reaching the river called the Tamesis, he searched for a crossing. His legions might have forded the river at low tide in the region of Westminster or further west at Brentford: his descriptions of the river and our knowledge of what it then looked like are too imprecise to be certain. But it was clearly not at the point where the Romans later chose to build a bridge, for the river here would have been too deep and too wide.

Caesar came and went without mentioning any place called Londinium, and without building a bridge. Almost a hundred years later a more concerted effort to subdue the Celtic tribes of Britain was made and this time the Romans established a route from the south coast which crossed the Thames at Westminster. The surviving pattern of roads shows this clearly. But there was still no bridge and the marshy banks of the Thames did not look promising for a permanent crossing. Instead the Romans are thought to have looked for a site further east suitable for a wooden bridge and, with this in view, chose a place where sandy islands on the south bank faced rising ground on the other side of the river. There is some evidence that this was the tidal limit of the Thames then, and a favourable place to land supplies.

The first bridge was completed around 47 AD and the military encampment on the north bank was established to defend it. The development of a port came later. This first Roman settlement had no defensive wall and was vulnerable to attack. According to legend it was pillaged and burned in 61 AD by Boudicca, leader of the Iceni tribe of East Anglia who had been incensed by the annexation of their territory and the treatment of her and her daughters at the hands of the Romans. Leading the whole of south-east England in revolt she was defeated in battle and committed suicide. The Romans re-established the settlement with improved defences. Around 100 AD a wall of regular stone blocks arose around the township enclosing 330 acres of land with the river as its southern boundary. This became known as 'The Square Mile', a term still used as a synonym for the City, London's financial centre.

Stone for the defensive wall around Londinium was not available locally. The Romans brought it from quarries on the tidal reaches of the River Medway, in Kent. Barges loaded with

Kentish ragstone would ride on the Medway tides out to the North Sea, sail up the east coast, and wait for the flood tide on the Thames to carry their cargoes up to Londinium. It was the beginning of the 'coasting trade' which was to be so important for London over the centuries. To bring such heavy loads over land with teams of oxen would have been much more time-consuming. The tidal Thames, linked by sea to another tidal river which could provide the building blocks of a new town, was vital to the city's development.

*The first London, built by the Romans, as it might have appeared from the air in the time of Hadrian around 120 AD. Artist Alan Sorrel has taken a perspective from the south-east, showing the Basilica and the Forum in the centre and the Walbrook stream, long hidden beneath the City streets, running into the Thames from the north. Londinium was not yet walled.*

Within the defensive wall the Romans established a classic provincial town which in time had a temple, bathhouses and a forum. Only recently, beneath the Guildhall, part of the wall of an amphitheatre, where entertainments were held and gladiators would have fought, was discovered and is now preserved under glass. By the early third century Londinium had become the Romans' provincial capital, with a thriving port where building materials, food and a host of goods were unloaded from galleys arriving from all parts of the east and south of England as well as from the Rhine and the Mediterranean. It was modern London in microcosm. But it did not last.

In 410 AD the Romans ceased to defend Britain as their empire crumbled and Rome itself became vulnerable to invaders from northern Europe. Archaeologists, excavating the layers of earth deposited over four centuries after the Romans left Londinium, have come to the conclusion that the city was abandoned. However, this ghost town was so sturdily built that a good deal of the structure survived, including the wall enclosing the square mile of the city.

# 3

# Lundenwic

~

Covent Garden, first laid out as a piazza in the seventeenth century by the architect Inigo Jones, is today a thriving district of shops and restaurants and home to the Royal Opera House. Visitors to the bustling streets get no sense that the River Thames is close by, just across the Strand. However, in Anglo-Saxon times, after the Romans had gone, the area which is now Covent Garden was open ground on the north bank of the Thames. It sloped down gently to the river's edge where traffic now roars along the Victoria Embankment.

From time to time, when the area of Covent Garden has been excavated for redevelopment, relics of an Anglo-Saxon settlement have been found there. They mostly date from about 500–600 AD, a time when the old Roman town appears to have been abandoned. During this period, the Anglo-Saxon people arrived in Britain from northern Europe and Scandinavia, bringing with them a Germanic language and a literature such as the unlettered Boudicca and the early Britons never had. But the Anglo-Saxons did not, on the whole, colonize abandoned Roman towns, preferring to establish their own, less sophisticated, settlements near by.

When, in 1994, a major extension was undertaken to Covent Garden Opera House, archaeologists had a chance to delve into the layers of history beneath. They found not only Anglo-Saxon pottery and other artefacts but a clear pattern of streets. This they were sure was the site of the settlement referred to in the *Anglo-Saxon Chronicle* as Lundenwic. Bede wrote of it as a bustling place with a lively trade along the Thames. Other finds were made when excavations were undertaken for the building of a new Jubilee Market in the Covent Garden piazza and archaeologists were able with some confidence to map the boundaries of Lundenwic, the name of Anglo-Saxon London.

These recent finds appear to have solved for good an age-old puzzle: how could Bede describe a thriving London when Roman London had clearly been abandoned? What he referred to was a new town quite different from Roman London, just a mile or so upriver. Lundenwic survived for perhaps three hundred years, though it was always vulnerable to attack. It had no bridge across to the south bank of the Thames and raiders could cruise in on the Thames tides and plunder its riches. The Vikings presented the greatest threat and their continual harassment persuaded the Anglo-Saxon king Alfred, in 886 AD, to move back into the ruins of Roman London and the protection of the old wall. Thereafter the settlement of Lundenwic appears to have been abandoned and was known as Aldwic – the old town.

When the area just to the east of the Strand was being redeveloped around 1900, an antiquarian suggested that a suitable name for the new crescent would be Aldwych to commemorate the former Thames-side settlement of the Anglo-Saxons. In fact the centre of old Lundenwic appears to have been below the Covent Garden piazza which was, until the 1970s, a famous market place for fruit and vegetables established in the mid-seventeenth century by the 5th Earl of Bedford.

Once the Anglo-Saxons moved back into Roman London the history of the city's development became one of almost continuous growth, with the river its vital lifeline. The position of London on the Thames was fixed for all time by the Anglo-Saxon desire to defend it from Viking invaders.

# 4

## Christianity

~

You can get a good idea of how much the landscape of the Thames has changed since Anglo-Saxon times by visiting Westminster Abbey. The Abbey stands well back from the Embankment, a view of the river obscured by the Victorian Gothic of the Houses of Parliament. Yet it arose on the site of a Benedictine monastery which had been built on an island, or 'eyot', known as Thornea close to the north bank of the Thames. There is disagreement among historians about the nature of this island. Some say it was formed by a fork in the Tyburn stream which ran into the Thames here, others say that it was just one of many sandy islands in the river.

Although some believe there was an earlier religious establishment on the site, the first written record is in a charter of King Offa around 785 AD which mentions 'St Peter and the people of the Lord dwelling in Thornea at the awesome place called Westminster'. There was a legend that St Peter himself had founded a monastery here, promising the locals a good catch of fish if they rowed him across the river. Offa, King of Mercia, was an early convert to Christianity.

The influence of the Christian church on the history of London has been profound. Although the first Christians would have arrived during the Roman occupation, they were banished to the west and north of the country by pagan invaders. In 597

Pope Gregory sent Augustine to southern Britain and, arriving at Thanet, he converted King Ethelbert of Kent, then the most powerful ruler in England, whose capital was not London but Canterbury. A bishopric was first established in London in 604, when the church of St Paul was founded on the site of the present cathedral. For the next two centuries London was disputed territory, and the influence of Christianity waxed and waned. By the tenth century the church was firmly established, with St Paul's (already burned and rebuilt more than once) the favoured place for the established ruler to worship.

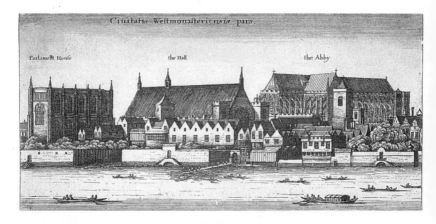

*An almost Venetian scene: Westminster Abbey and the old Parliament buildings to the north of the Thames in 1647. The artist, Wenceslaus Hollar, shows the busy activity of the watermen when the river was still London's main highway for all social classes. When the first religious houses were established here they were on an island which disappeared long ago as London grew.*

It was Edward the Confessor, ruler from 1042 to the momentous year of 1066, who first took royalty to Westminster, rebuilding the Abbey which is featured in the Norman Bayeux Tapestry. Edward had a mausoleum built here, and William the Conqueror had himself crowned in the Abbey after his defeat of Harold at the Battle of Hastings in 1066. From that time on, the Abbey of St Peter in the west became the focus of political power, and St Paul's in the east the focus of the City's commerce and trade, the two linked by the Thames which was the main highway of London. In the sixteenth century some of the money collected for the upkeep and building of Westminster Abbey (dedicated to St Peter) was transferred to the coffers of St Paul's – probably the origin of the expression 'robbing Peter to pay Paul'. Whereas Westminster Abbey has been added to over the centuries, St Paul's was entirely rebuilt after the Great Fire of 1666.

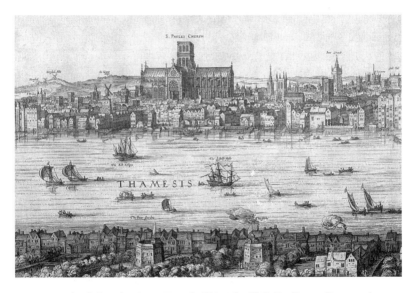

*London before the Great Fire of 1666 with old St Paul's standing proud on the north of the river, on a site where the first church was established as early as 604. This engraving by Vischer dates from 1616.*

On the south bank of the Thames there are two other great ecclesiastical buildings, Lambeth Palace and Lambeth Church, which have later origins than either the Abbey or the Cathedral. They are, it seems, on the wrong side of the river, cut off from the twin centres of Westminster and the City. The land was first acquired by the church in the twelfth century by Baldwin, Archbishop of Canterbury, who intended to build there a college for monks. This scheme apparently came to nothing, but by 1197 a house had been built which became the official residence of the Archbishops of Canterbury. A ferry which could carry a coach and horses was established to link Lambeth with Westminster, handy for the Archbishops both for their own trips into town and for the toll charges which gave them a substantial income. The Lambeth horse ferry had a chequered history, about which more later.

*Lambeth Palace in the late eighteenth century. The official residence of the Archbishops of Canterbury has been on this site from 1197, and until Westminster Bridge was opened in 1750 the quickest way across the river to the Court and Parliament was by the Palace 'horse ferry' which could carry carriages as well as foot passengers.*

# 5

## Old London Bridge

~

The London Bridge you can walk across today is constructed of prestressed concrete, spans the river on three arches and was completed in 1972. It bears no resemblance at all to the historic Old London Bridge which stood just to the east of the present bridge, from its completion in 1209 until it was demolished in 1831. This first stone bridge spanned the river on nineteen arches, each of which was supported by two 'starlings', boat-shaped breakwaters which cut through the force of the tides and river flow. For five centuries the narrow roadway of Old London Bridge was like a tunnel between the shops, houses and chapel built along its length.

No modern pleasure boat would have been able to pass under any of the arches of Old London Bridge. There was, for a long time, a small drawbridge near the centre and tall ships could pass through it if they paid a toll. But, in effect, the bridge was a barrier dividing the tidal Thames, where ocean-going vessels moored, from the upper reaches of the river. In effect, Old London Bridge held back the flow of flood tides.

As you stand on London Bridge today you might wonder why a city which was reliant on river transport would make the decision to construct at huge expense such a formidable obstacle to shipping. The answer, most historians now believe, is that it was not built primarily as a river crossing. Whereas for the Romans the bridge at Londinium provided a short cut from the Kent coast to East Anglia and northern England, for the Anglo-Saxons, and later the Normans, the purpose of a bridge was different. The wooden bridges built by the Saxons were clearly intended as a defensive

*A section of Old London Bridge around 1600, showing the continuous wall of houses and shops and the narrowness of the arches which formed a barrier across the Thames. Most of that part of the bridge shown here was destroyed by fire in 1632.*

barrier across the river to repel invaders sailing up the Thames from the east coast. In 994 AD the Vikings burned and ransacked London. Sometime after this the Saxons, having regained possession of the town, built their first wooden bridge across the river.

Lying just upstream of the Roman bridge, the earliest remnants so far found, dating from 1000 AD, suggest that it was like a barrage lying low over the water so that no ships could be rowed under it.

But the Vikings and their allies continued to invade and this bridge was torn down in 1014 AD. According to one account given in the Norse legends known as the Olaf sagas, they rowed up to it, tied ropes to the piers and then set off downstream, carried no doubt by the ebb tide, taking the wooden bridge with them. Many people believe this to be the ancient origin of the children's nursery rhyme 'London Bridge is falling down'. However, that was not the only disaster to befall the wooden Saxon bridges – one was washed away by high tides, others simply collapsed. Until the arrival of the Normans and the building of a sturdier structure, London Bridge kept on falling down.

When the last of the Saxon kings, Edward the Confessor, died in January 1066 the battle to succeed him was decisive. His nominee Harold, fighting to retain the crown, was defeated at Hastings by Duke William of Normandy. London held out for a time, refusing to allow William to cross the bridge from Southwark. But in the end the City submitted and the Normans under William ('the Conqueror') began their long campaign to subdue all of England, building the first substantial stone castles and walls since the retreat of the Romans. When London Bridge had to be replaced, the decision to build it in stone presented a formidable challenge: with the technology then available there was no question of spanning the Thames with two or three elegant arches. But as the bridge was almost certainly regarded as part of London's defences, like a long arm thrown across the river from the City to hold back riverborne attack, the fact that it presented an obstacle to shipping was not considered to be a problem.

It took thirty years to build Old London Bridge and cost a fortune. Money was raised by a special tax on wool exports and many made bequests to 'God and the Bridge'. To pay for the cost of upkeep, houses and shops were built on it, the rents going to

a bridge fund – except on occasions when the income was pur-
loined by kings in search of a ready source of cash. The roadway
between the buildings was only twenty feet wide, another indication that the first purpose of the bridge was not to make it
easier to cross the Thames.

When the tide was running, water raced through the arches
of Old London Bridge as if tumbling over a weir. It could bank
up several feet higher on one side than the other. The arches
were not of even dimensions and the watermen who learned to
'shoot the bridge' like white water canoeists, gave names to each
of the treacherous openings: Long Entry, Chapel Lock, Gut
Lock, Rock Lock and, the largest where there was a drawbridge,
Draw Lock. When the tide was high, clearance for a boat shooting the lowest lock could be down to eight feet. On the turn of
the tide the watermen would gather, awaiting their moment to
get washed through, and they often had good sport rowing after
livestock that tumbled from the bridge. So treacherous was the
rush of water through the arches that, at one time, one of the
shops on the bridge above specialized in selling cork life jackets.

One of the wonders of medieval Europe, Old London Bridge
ensured over the centuries that the bulk of the nation's wealth
accumulated in the City. Ships carrying goods brought from
around the world moored just below the bridge, creating a busy
and ever more congested seaport. Coal, wheat, quarry stone,
timber brought from around the coast was also routed to London
Bridge, and much of it was taxed, swelling the coffers of the City
and its merchants. Upkeep of the bridge was paid for out of a
trust and the City staunchly opposed the building of any new
bridges upriver which might threaten its age-old monopoly.

The opening of Westminster Bridge in 1750 sealed the fate of
Old London Bridge. Southwark on the south bank was by then
a thriving part of the metropolis and the City recognized that
Old London Bridge would have to become a bridge proper

rather than an extension of London built over the river. The shops and houses would have to come down – most of them anyway were in poor repair despite some extensive rebuilding programmes. In the autumn of 1757 a temporary wooden bridge

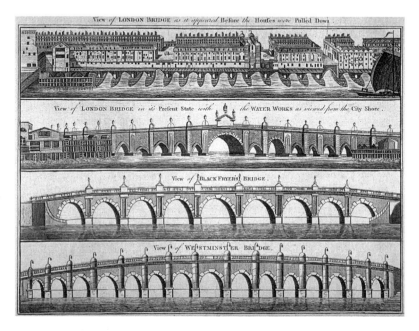

*The opening of Westminster Bridge (bottom) in 1750 broke the monopoly of Old London Bridge (top) as a river crossing. To make it easier for traffic to cross London Bridge the houses and shops were taken down and it was 'modernized' with fewer arches (second picture down). Having lost the battle to stop the rival Westminster Bridge scheme, the City began to build more bridges of its own, the first of which was Blackfriars Bridge opened in 1769 (third from top).*

was built alongside the old bridge so that traffic could still cross while the buildings were being taken down. But this bridge was severely damaged by fire and the demolition work had to be speeded up. Compensation was paid to those who lost their properties and toll charges were brought in to defray the cost – even the watermen had to pay for risking their lives shooting the bridge. The tolls were very unpopular and were lifted in 1758 when Parliament helped to bail the City out of its plight.

A wider opening, which became known as the Great Arch, was made in London Bridge and Thames tides began to flow through it more freely than they had done for over a thousand years. They were anyway pushing further inland now as the south-east of England tilted seaward and embanking of the river with wooden timbers for wharves prevented the flood tide from spreading as it raced in. When Old London Bridge was demolished entirely and replaced in August 1831 by a new bridge just a little upstream, the old barrier was gone and the tides raced even further inland. The City, now immensely wealthy, could afford to get rid of the old barrier and allow the river traffic to flow. Great docklands had already been built to the east to ease the pressure on the Pool of London, and there had been a spate of bridge building, some of it funded by the City itself.

The bridge of 1831, designed by the father and son team of architects John Rennie, lasted until 1968, when it was taken down stone by stone and shipped across the Atlantic. It was bought by Robert McCulloch, a chainsaw magnate, and reassembled at Lake Havasu City in western Arizona. Many thought the price he paid, $2.4 million, was exorbitant. But it has become a great tourist attraction, spanning a lagoon by Lake Havasu as the centrepiece of a new development which includes a 'London village' and a local radio station KBBC, which styles itself 'BBC radio'.

# 6

## Frost Fairs

~

The last time the Thames froze in London was during an exceptionally long, cold spell in the winter of 1962–3. But there was no question of anyone getting their skates out and cutting a dash on the ice, even less the possibility of a winter fair on the frozen river. For a long time the tides have been too strong and the climate too warm for a repetition of the fantastic impromptu 'frost fairs' of earlier centuries. The last was held in the winter of 1813–14, a few years before Old London Bridge was pulled down. For it was the Old Bridge, just as much as the colder climate, which had made the fairs possible; with the flow of the river above the bridge held back by the arches, it was much easier for the Thames to freeze. But, spectacular though they were when they were held, frost fairs were rare events. The first recorded fair was held in the winter of 1564–5, the second more than a century later in 1683–4; others followed in 1715–16, 1739–40 and, finally, 1813–14. In 1789 there was a huge fair upriver from London Bridge at Putney.

Londoners did not venture on to the ice in numbers until there had been more than a week of continuous frost and they could be confident the river was frozen to a depth which would support the weight of thousands of people. Two days before Christmas 1683 the Thames was frozen across and on New Year's Day 1684 streets of tent-like booths appeared on the ice and formed an avenue which was instantly named Temple Street, as it ran from the Temple Stairs where watermen waited for passengers. Horse-drawn carriages were able to cross the ice and a bullring was set up close to London Bridge. Watermen, desperate for trade,

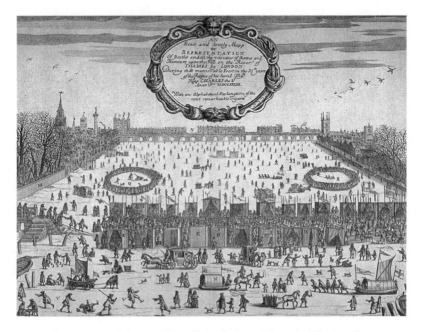

*A panorama of the great Frost Fair of 1683–4 when the Thames above London Bridge froze solid. Watermen turned their wherries into sledges or put them on wheels, oxen were roasted on the river and there were booths for entertainment and food.*

hitched their boats to horses and sleighed up and down the river. A printing press was set up on the ice and the diarist John Evelyn noted:

The people and ladies took a fancy to have their names printed, and the day and year set down when printed on the Thames: this humour took so universally, that it is estimated the printer gained £5 a day, for printing a line only, at sixpence a name, besides that he got by ballads etc.

Charles II, his brother James, Duke of York, and Queen Catherine, Infanta of Portugal, all had their names printed on the frozen Thames. A ballad commemorated the wonders of 'Freezeland Street' where you could buy all kinds of goods, cloth and pots, as well as food and drink. There was bull-baiting on the ice, along with horse and coach races, and puppet shows. Oxen were roasted without making much impression on the solid ice, which remained frozen for about a month so that the booths and festivities extended further and further from the bridge and sightseers rode in coaches from one end to the other.

One of the longest spells of freezing weather began in December 1739 and lasted through until February. But there was a sudden thaw in between. A Frost Fair had begun on Christmas Day and by 21 January a large number of stalls was set out above the bridge. Overnight the weather warmed and an extraordinary scene greeted the people who lived on the west side of the bridge when they awoke the following morning. According to the *Universal Spectator*:

> on opening their windows there appeared underneath on the river a parcel of booths, shops and huts of different forms, but without any inhabitants. Here stood a booth with trinkets, here a hut with a Dram of Old Gold, in another place a skittle frame and pins, and in a fourth 'The Noble Art and Mystery of Printing'.

All the stalls had drifted into each other in the thaw, and then frozen again in a jumble. However, the Frost Fair continued until 14 February when the Thames suddenly dissolved and smashed ice into the bridge which was badly damaged.

Ice on the Thames often inflicted more damage than it offered amusement. During the winter of 1763–4 the water between all but one of the piers froze solid so that the entire force of the river was concentrated on the remaining arch. The rush of water so scoured the river bed that it undermined the foundations of the bridge. Again in 1813–14, when the days of Old London Bridge were clearly numbered, the last great Frost Fair ended in a sudden thaw which drowned many people and smashed ice and roaring water into the piers. Repairing the damage was extremely costly and the City finally took the decision to build a new bridge. Although the Thames froze again on occasions, there were no more Frost Fairs: the tides flowed freely under the new bridge of 1831, so no great depth of ice formed even in bitter winters.

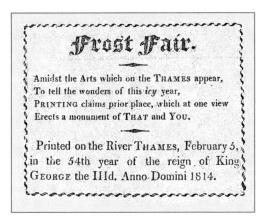

*Frost fairs were rare even before the nineteenth century and were never held again after Old London Bridge came down in the 1830s because the flow of the tides was no longer checked sufficiently for thick ice to form. This is a memento of the last fair held in 1814.*

# 7

# The Tower of London

~

What is striking today about the Tower of London, seen from a riverboat or from Tower Bridge, is how small-scale it looks, like a child's model castle. Dwarfed now by the great tower blocks that rise close to it in the City it seems almost unbelievably quaint and hardly suggests awe-inspiring impregnability or political power. Yet in its day it was an immensely impressive structure which owed the strength of its stone walls, some of them fifteen feet thick, to its favourable site on the Thames. William the Conqueror was a ruler in a largely hostile country and to secure his position built a series of strongholds, the first of which was on the site of the Tower. It was a makeshift timber fort at first, providing a defence against the continuing threat of invasion from Scandinavians sailing up the Thames as well as a safeguard against potentially rebellious subjects. There were two other forts begun in the years following the Conquest, both close to the river: Baynard's Castle on the east bank of the Fleet river where it ran into the Thames, and Montfichet at Ludgate. But it was the Tower into which William put his impressive resources.

The first stage of permanent building, just outside the old Roman wall, was finished sometime after 1087. It is constructed of a distinctive light-coloured stone which the Norman builders imported from Caen in Normandy. What became known as the White Tower is over ninety feet high with immense walls all the stone for which was shipped across the English Channel and up the Thames. It was not just the tidal nature of the river which made this possible: the prevailing south-westerlies on the Channel would have given the ships carrying the building blocks of the Tower fair winds. This white tower of Caen stone, which has survived very nearly a millennium, was added to over a long period of time to form the walled citadel of today.

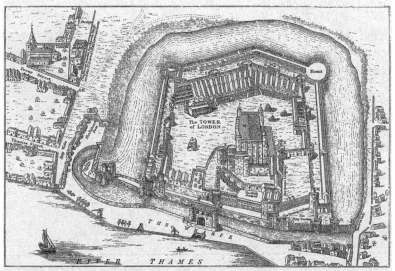

THE TOWER. (From a Survey made in 1597 by W. Haiward and J. Gascoyne.)

A. Middle Tower. B. Tower at the Gate. C. Bell Tower. D. Beauchamp Tower. E. Devilin Tower. F. Flint Tower. G. Bowyer Tower. H. Brick Tower. I. Martin Tower. K. Constable Tower. L. Broad Arrow Tower. M. Salt Tower. N. Well Tower. O. Tower leading to Iron Gate. P. Tower above Iron Gate. Q. Cradle Tower. R. Lantern Tower. S. Hall Tower. T. Bloody Tower. V. St. Thomas's Tower. W. Cæsar's, or White Tower. X. Cole Harbour. Y. Wardrobe Tower. A B. House at Water Gate, called the Ram's Head. A H. End of Tower Street.

*The Tower of London as it was in 1597, a fortress just to the east of the City with direct access to the river by what became known as Traitor's Gate. Much of the stone for the building was shipped across the Channel from Caen in France, and carried upstream on the Thames tides.*

The significance of the Tower in London's history has been obscured by centuries of secrecy and romanticization. In fact no other historic building in the country has been subject to such an accumulation of myth and obfuscation and it is only recently that diligent research has made some sense of what historians regard as a hopelessly popularized 'heritage monster' with its theatrical Beefeaters and blood-curdling tours. That it was always a fortress is not in doubt. But it was also a palace, and for a time a place of refuge for monarchs who could sail straight from the Thames into their private rooms through a tunnel. It was the place where kings and queens kept their menagerie of exotic beasts – among them Henry III's polar bear, a gift from the King of Norway in 1252, which the sheriffs of London provided with collar and chain so it could fish in the river. The Tower was also a safe where the valuable accoutrements of royalty, the so-called 'Crown Jewels', were stored for safe keeping. After Oliver Cromwell had had Charles I executed, most of the regalia associated with the monarchy were destroyed. A new set was made for Charles II's coronation.

The Tower was also a kind of police station with a stock of arms and a Constable in charge ready to suppress faction and riot among rebellious subjects. A considerable armoury was held there until the 1860s as a safeguard against insurrection in London. But the Tower became most famous, or notorious, as a prison in which hapless captives, both guilty and innocent, were locked away never to see the light of day again before their execution.

Until 1810 the Tower housed the Royal Mint which designed and cast coinage, and the menagerie survived until 1835 when the last remaining wild creatures were transferred to the new zoo in Regent's Park. Exactly when the last prisoners were held there is not clear but it seems there were none between the Battle of Waterloo in 1815 and the First World War, when the Irish nationalist Sir Roger Casement was incarcerated in the Tower, charged with planning the Easter Rising of 1916, for which he was condemned to death and hanged.

In the 1830s and 1840s there were many romantic books written about the Tower. They mixed fact and fiction and greatly increased popular interest in it. Yet to get in you had to pay a high fee or be given a special ticket. Once inside, the Yeomen – members of a royal bodyguard of veterans – would demand another hefty fee. Throughout the nineteenth century there was a clamour to open the Tower up to the public and to do away with charges. The annual number of visitors rose from around 10,000 in 1800 to nearly half a million in 1900, by which time entrance was free and what remained of the contents of the Tower had been organized into exhibits of various kinds. The hordes who flocked there were most interested in the dungeons and the 'thumbscrews', and the Tower's store of ghoulish tales of murder and execution.

Today you have to pay to visit the Tower of London, yet there are more than 2.5 million visitors from around the world each year soaking up the atmosphere of what appears to be a kind of historical theme park. Though it stands right on the river, the Tower's close association with the Thames disappeared centuries ago and it is best seen as representative of the scale and nature of the city when Old London Bridge stood proud, holding back the tides.

# 8

# Stairs and wherries

⌒

Despite the heavy traffic congestion on London's central roads today, anyone in a hurry to get from the City to Whitehall would hail a black cab and hope for the best. Making the same journey in the winter of 1667, Samuel Pepys noted in his diary: 'By coach to the Temple, and then for speed by water thence to Whitehall.' It says something about the state of the roads in seventeenth-century London that Pepys should have found it quicker to clamber down the watermen's 'stairs' halfway through his journey and climb into a rowing boat, than ask the coachman to carry him to Whitehall. As a government official Pepys had available to him his own barge with liveried watermen, though on the occasion mentioned in 1667 he probably jumped from his coach and took the first wherry available. In fact he was probably surrounded by competing watermen shouting: 'Oars!'

That cry was familiar to Londoners for hundreds of years, disappearing only in the early twentieth century when finally the bridging of the river, the wash of steamboats and the rivalry of new roads put the watermen out of business. They had been the city's taxi drivers since the Middle Ages, cockney gondoliers whose repartee and raucous clamour for custom greatly impressed foreign visitors. A young Frenchman, César de Saussure, wrote home in 1725:

You cannot see anything more delightful than this river. Above the Bridge it is covered with craft of every sort; round about London there are at least 15,000 boats for the transport of persons . . . Nothing is more attractive than the Thames on a fine summer evening; the conversations you hear are most entertaining, for I must tell you that it is the custom for anyone on the water to call out whatever he pleases to other occupants of boats, even were I the King himself, and no one has the right to be shocked . . . Most bargemen are very skilful in this mode of warfare using singular and quite extraordinary terms, generally very coarse and dirty and I cannot possibly explain them to you.

*A couple heading by wherry for a night out at Vauxhall pleasure gardens around 1790, when the Thames was still an important highway in London. All along the shore there were 'stairs' like these, where the rough-tongued watermen plied for trade. The saucy caption to this picture reads:* 'Be cautious my love . . . don't expose your leg.'

These boats are very attractive and cleanly kept, and are light in weight, painted generally in red or green, and can hold six persons comfortably. On rainy days they are covered with coarse strong tents and in the summer when the sun is burning hot, with an awning of thin green or red woollen stuff . . . The boatmen wear a peculiar kind of cap made of velvet or black plush, and sometimes of cloth the same colour as their waistcoats. As soon as a person approaches the stairs they run to meet him calling out lustily 'Oars, oars' or 'Sculler, sculler'. They continue this melodious music until the person points with his finger to the man he has chosen, and they at once unite in abusive language at the offending boatman.

As well as ferrying Londoners across the river they took Pepys and others up and down the Thames, with most of their trade along the densely built-up north bank. The distances they rowed, often against the tide, were prodigious. One celebrated trip in the early 1700s is still commemorated today in a watermen's contest on the river, the Doggett's Coat and Badge race. Thomas Doggett was an actor who often performed at Drury Lane, a long way from his home in Chelsea. In his three-volume *History of the Watermen's Company* (published 1874–86), Henry Humpherus gives an account of the origins of the race for newly qualified watermen.

Mr Doggett being at one of the Stairs, wished to hire a waterman to row him up the river home, but it being a bad night and against tide, the men demurred doing so – a young waterman at length offered his services, and having accomplished the journey, Mr Doggett found on enquiry that he had only just got his freedom of the company [that is, finished his apprenticeship] and was very deserving of support, he therefore well rewarded him for his trouble and established this match; it being the means also of commemorating the accession of the House of Hanover to the Throne of England.

The first race was rowed in 1715, the winner getting prize money and an orange coat and badge emblazoned with the

White Horse of Hanover (George I came to the throne in 1714, the first of the Hanoverian dynasty that reigned until 1837). It was a tough race rowed against the tide from the Swan Inn at London Bridge to the Swan Inn at Chelsea. The wherries then in use were not racers and were much heavier going than the light craft used in the race today, which is rowed *with* the tide. It is no longer only for apprentice watermen: from the 1950s non-professionals were allowed to compete.

In his *Survey of London* published in 1598 the chronicler and antiquary John Stow estimated that there were 40,000 licensed watermen on the river – an impression rather than a hard statistic but some indication of how central the Thames was to London life. For a long time the watermen who rowed goods on the river and those who took passengers were in dispute, accusing each other of stealing trade, but their two companies were merged in 1700 and the qualifications became the same.

The arrival of the horse-drawn carriage in London in 1565 was the first threat to the livelihood of the watermen, who complained continually that private and public coaches were taking their custom and causing a nuisance by jamming the narrow roads. In 1633 they persuaded the Star Chamber to issue an order forbidding coachmen to wait outside a playhouse at Blackfriars for theatregoers while a production was on, threatening to throw them in Newgate or Ludgate prisons if they disobeyed. It was far better for those going to a play to take a wherry or to walk. The 'water poet' John Taylor, a West Country lad who became a waterman, penned a memorable verse pleading the case against rival road traffic:

> Carroaches, coaches, jades and Flanders mares
> Doe rob us of our shares, our wares, our fares,
> Against the ground we stand and knock our heeles
> Whilst all our profits run away on wheels . . .

Taylor, who was later press-ganged into the Navy, wrote his lament in 1622. For a further three centuries the watermen con-

tinued to ply for hire, disputing every new-fangled development
in London transport. They especially opposed all new bridge
building which not only made things easier for road traffic, but
made their own job much harder because of the tug of the tides
around the arches and the often low clearance when the water
was high. But there were still 1,600 watermen when the journalist Henry Mayhew went out to collect their stories in 1849–50
for his *Morning Chronicle* pieces, later collected as *London Labour
and the London Poor*. One waterman explained their plight:

> people may talk as they like about what's been the ruin of us –
> it's nothing but new London Bridge. When my old father heard
> that the old bridge was to come down, 'Bill' he says, 'it'll be up
> with the watermen in no time.' If the old bridge had stood how
> would all these steamers have got through it all. At some tides, it
> was so hard to shoot London Bridge that people wouldn't trust
> themselves to any but watermen. Now any fool might manage.
> London Bridge, Sir, depend on it, has ruined us.

In 1815, the first Thames steamer, the *Margery*, began a pioneer
service below Old London Bridge, taking passengers from
Wapping to Gravesend. The *Margery* did not strike the watermen as much of a threat: they nicknamed it 'the Yankee
Torpedo' after an American steamer that had blown up. The
*Margery* was a comical vessel which had its paddles, shaped
rather like duck's feet, at the back. It was slow – the journey to
Gravesend took on average more than five hours – and its
paddles continually snapped. However, by the 1840s more
streamlined and efficient steamers became popular. To begin
with, the watermen had plenty of work rowing passengers out
to them, but in time the steamer companies built piers and took
away that trade. Worst of all, the paddle steamers created wash
which tossed the watermen's wherries about uncomfortably. A
waterman complained to Mayhew in 1850 that a woman passenger refused to get in his wherry when she saw the wash of

a steamer going by; as a result he lost a two shilling fare and waited five hours for his next customer.

However, even in the late nineteenth century with the river bridged all the way through London and the steamers crowding the river, the watermen were still a feature of the river scene. In *Dickens's Dictionary of the Thames* published in 1890 (the work of the celebrated novelist's son, also called Charles) watermen's fares are listed for many river journeys. 'From London-bridge, above the said bridge, to Southwark-bridge, Oars 6d Sculler 3d . . . From London-bridge, above the said bridge, to Waterloo-bridge, Oars 1s 6d Sculler 9d . . .' and so on. You could get a wherry or some other craft all the way down to Greenwich and all the way up to Chelsea Bridge. In fact the watermen would take you anywhere they could reach on the river at an agreed rate per mile, with luggage too, up to a limit of 56lb in weight.

As well as the workaday wherries moored alongside the hundred or so riverside 'stairs' on the Thames in London, there were royal and ceremonial barges with gilt frames and ornate canopies – Rolls-Royces of the river – housed in boatsheds ashore. From the mid-fifteenth century members of the City livery companies which controlled trade and industry acquired their own barges, the first belonging to Sir John Norman, a draper whose watermen were supplied with silver oars. The livery company barges were seen to best effect in the annual Lord Mayor's Show, a pageant in which the newly elected Mayor of the City presented himself to the Law Courts and Westminster and processed back to the Guildhall. From 1422 part of the journey took place on the Thames, the livery companies hiring watermen's boats. By the sixteenth century they all had their own barges and decked them out lavishly. One seventeenth-century procession included five islands created on the river 'artfully garnished with all manner of Indian fruit trees, drugges, spiceries and the like, the middle island having a faire castle especially beautified'.

The Lord Mayor's Show continued on the river until 1856, by which time the stench of sewage was so bad it was driven on to land and the barges were sold off. Oxford and Cambridge Universities bought them to use as boat houses. Those destined for Cambridge were rowed down the estuary and out on to the North Sea heading for the River Cam, but they did not make it. The whole lot sank off the east coast.

The royal state barge lasted longer than those of the livery companies. That built in 1689 for William III had its last outing on the Thames at the 1919 peace pageant following the end of the First World War. The fraternity of King's (or Queen's) watermen did not however lose their jobs. After centuries of railing against the depredations of road travel they negotiated an amphibious deal whereby they acquired the right to ride the royal coach. It is still their job to deliver the crown to Westminster during the ceremony of the State Opening of Parliament. Otherwise, the few surviving watermen work the tourist boats, the tugs which haul rubbish barges, and other craft like the *Thames Champion* which makes constant checks on the flood defences. None wields an oar, everything is motorized, but knowledge of the swirl of the tides as the Thames races under bridges remains a specialist skill, and the watermen still have their company and their hall in the City.

# 9

# The Prospect of Whitby

~

One of the most famous of London's riverside pubs is the Prospect of Whitby tucked away in Wapping in the heart of the old port. It is an odd name for a dockland inn as Whitby is a fishing port far up the east coast of England a long way out of sight of the Thames. What it commemorates, however, is a trade which sustained London for centuries: the shipping of coal from the mines of north-eastern England and Scotland. The old inn itself dates from the sixteenth century but it was renamed towards the end of the eighteenth century after a ship which was one of hundreds of sailing colliers which moored in the river below London Bridge. *The Prospect of Whitby* was built in Whitby, in north Yorkshire, in 1777 and was lost in a storm in the Bay of Biscay in 1795 on a voyage to the Mediterranean after serving its time carrying coal to London.

Exactly when in history London was no longer able to warm itself in winter and fuel its ovens and factories with firewood and charcoal cannot be dated exactly, but it is evident that woodland supplies must have been running short even in the fourteenth century. That is when the first importation of coal from northeast England is recorded. It was known as 'sea coal' to distinguish it from charcoal which at the time was known simply as 'coal'. (The term may have originally referred to coal that was washed up on the beaches of north-eastern England before mining became extensive.)

There has been much argument among antiquarians about exactly how and where north-eastern coal was unloaded and sold in London. One possibility is that it was first taken into the tidal mouth of the River Fleet where it joined the Thames, more or less where Blackfriars Bridge stands now. The tidal water pushed into a creek over which Farringdon Road was built, and from the east bank ran a cobbled passage called Old Seacoal Lane, now swallowed up in new developments. Other records of the time suggest that coal was delivered to an area known as Romeland at Billingsgate, where the coal factors struck deals with the collier ship captains. From the early days a duty was charged on coal, which provided an income for the City, and as early as the thirteenth century complaints were heard about air pollution from coal fires.

So much is made of the more exotic traffic of the Thames – the spices and luxury goods brought in by the merchant companies from India and China – that the workaday business of keeping the capital fuelled is often forgotten. Today, nearly half a century after a law banned the burning of coal in London hearths and factories, it is difficult to imagine how dependent the capital was on collier ships from the days of Samuel Pepys in the 1660s to the Beatlemania of the 1960s. The poet John Cleveland made the point nicely in a verse penned in 1650:

> England's a perfect world, hath Indies too,
> Correct your maps, Newcastle is Peru.

The coal trade between the north-east of England and London had far more than local significance. Daniel Defoe, author of *Robinson Crusoe*, wrote in his *Tour through the Whole Island of Great Britain*, published in 1724:

I need not, except for the sake of strangers, take notice that the City of London and parts adjacent . . . is supplied with coals, therefore called sea coal, from Newcastle upon Tyne and from the coast of Durham and Northumberland . . . All these coals are bought and sold on this little spot of Room Land at Billingsgate and though sometimes, especially in the case of war and contrary winds, a fleet of five hundred to seven hundred sail of ships comes up the river at a time, yet they never want for a market . . . This trade is so considerable it is esteemed a nursery of our best seamen.

One of those seamen was none other than Captain James Cook who sailed around the world twice in the 1760s and '70s before his unfortunate end in 1779, bludgeoned and stabbed to death in the surf on a Hawaiian beach after an argument with the islanders. Cook, the son of a Yorkshire farmer, learned his seamanship on the collier run from Whitby to London, and the ship he took on his first world voyage was a collier, refitted and renamed the *Endeavour*. Less fortunate sailors on the collier ships were the favourite target for the press-gangs that stalked the inns and lodging houses of the old port in search of likely victims for forced service in the British Navy.

Coal shipped up the Thames is a rich seam in London's history. When the first railways were built, from the 1830s, some of the supplies previously brought from the north by canal or down the east coast shifted to the coal wagons hauled by steam trains. But the seaborne coal trade was so well established it continued to grow as London expanded with the building booms of the Victorian period. The autumn and winter fogs that provided the atmospheric soup for many episodes in the novels of Charles Dickens were the creation of hundreds of thousands of factory chimneys and home fires. The journalist Henry Mayhew, who had a predilection for statistics, estimated that in 1861 the northeast collier ships – 2,717 of them manned by 21,600 sailors – delivered nearly three and a half million tons of coal to London. All of this was unloaded from ships to lighters by teams of 'coal whippers' who, four at a time, heaved on ropes to raise a basket of coal which was then tipped down a shute.

By the turn of the twentieth century the railways were bringing in much of the domestic coal and polluting industries were
being driven out of the built-up areas of London. But a new
development kept London dependent on coal from the north-
east: electricity. All the earliest power stations were hydroelectric
– Lord Salisbury lit his country seat, Hatfield House, with power
from a generator turned by a tributary of the Thames, the River
Lea, in the 1880s – or coal fired. They had to be sited locally as
there was no national grid to distribute power over long distances
as there is today. When the American financier Charles Tyson
Yerkes arrived in London in 1901 intent on creating a new transport system for the capital, electrification of trains and trams was
the rage. Yerkes put together a company called the Underground
Group and raised money for the building of the earliest sections
of the Bakerloo, Piccadilly and Northern lines. He also
electrified the District Line which, along with the Metropolitan
and Circle lines, had been steam driven. To provide the power
for his enterprise he had built to American specifications a gen-
erating station at Lots Road in Chelsea. It took three years to
build and when it went into service in 1905 it was the largest
power station in Europe.

Lots Road was sited on the Thames so that its fuel could be
delivered by boat from the north-east and river water could be
drawn in to cool the system. A huge drain was created in the
river bed so that when the cover was hoisted a whirlpool
appeared where the water was sucked down and into the power
station. Lots Road survived until 2002 when it was decommis-
sioned and work began to convert it into a new and fashionable
enclave of artistic Chelsea.

After 1905 power stations began to appear all along the river.
The London County Council built a giant structure at
Greenwich to provide electricity for its trams and, though the
trams disappeared long ago, the station is still in operation, providing some of the power for the underground. The most

famous power station of all was Battersea, completed in 1932 to the design of Giles Gilbert Scott; its four brick chimneys are as much a landmark as Tower Bridge or the twin towers of Wembley Stadium to the north. Others followed at Fulham, Woolwich and Bankside, all rising like windowless castles on the river to light up London as the capital gradually got rid of its gas lighting and switched to electricity.

Delivering coal to Greenwich was not difficult as there were no bridges across the river up to that point. But getting upstream to Fulham, Battersea and Chelsea presented a problem. The ingenious solution was the 'flattie' or 'flat-iron', a barge-like cargo boat which lay low in the water and had a folding funnel. When sailing from Newcastle upon Tyne fully loaded with coal, the flat-iron was barely visible above the surface of the sea and they were called sardonically 'north-east submarines' by the sailors who manned them. Coming up to London on the flood tide they would hit top speed as, even with their funnels down, they could only just get under the bridges as the water level rose. Westminster Bridge was the worst and on occasion they only made it because the flat-iron momentarily displaced the water under the arches as they went through. Sometimes they miscalculated and became wedged, a nice prize for the Thames tugboat men who claimed a handsome fee for salvaging them.

The coal trade on the Thames continued into the 1960s, by which time the Clean Air Act of 1956 which banned the burning of coal had begun to take effect, the power stations had converted to oil or gas, and the chimneys of London homes no longer smoked on winter evenings. The fogs disappeared in the early 1960s and lichen began to grow again on London's parkland and street trees. But the legacy of the coal trade is still there all along the river. After years of deliberation and failed schemes, Battersea Power Station is being revamped with hotels, theatres and restaurants, Bankside houses the Tate Modern art gallery and Lots Road will soon be another Thames-side attraction.

# 10

# The Great Fire and after

~

What the view of the City would be like today from the Millennium Bridge if a large part of its seventeenth-century fabric had not been either burned to the ground or blown up in an effort to halt the flames of the Great Fire of 1666 it is impossible to say. It would certainly have been rebuilt at some later period, but the old St Paul's Cathedral, for which a major renovation was planned by the architect Sir Christopher Wren just before the fire, might well have survived along with some of the City's other churches.

As it happened, there arose from the ashes of the conflagration a much finer city of churches and streets than the fire had consumed. Only six people are known to have died in the fire, though there might have been more. As it burned for five days there was time for most people to rescue their belongings, many of them taking to the river. It was a stupendous blaze, dutifully recorded by, among others, the remarkable draughtsman from Bohemia Wenceslaus Hollar who was working in London at the time. But it was not, in the long run, a catastrophe for London, which recovered with remarkable speed.

In the years immediately before the Great Fire, London had had a very tough time. The Plague of 1665 had inflicted a horrible death on thousands, whilst marauding Dutch ships during the continuing Anglo-Dutch wars had disrupted the delivery of

coal from the north-east of England as well as of building stone from Kent and the quarries along the south coast. The French were a constant threat too, and there were widespread rumours, some endorsed by the House of Commons, that the fire had been started by Papists, the same Catholic terrorists who had tried to blow up Parliament in the Gunpowder Plot of 1605.

An unfortunate watchmaker from Rouen, Robert Hubert, was caught apparently fleeing the country and was forced to confess to starting the fire. He was said to have been seen pushing incendiary material through the window of the baker's house in Pudding Lane where the fire began. Though no such window existed and most level-headed commentators thought all conspiracy theories groundless, hapless Hubert was condemned and hanged at Tyburn, the gallows on the edge of the stream of that name which once flowed on a route down Park Lane.

Though suspicions about French conspirators took a long time to die, the second Anglo-Dutch war ended in 1667 and Thames trade was re-established. A new range of taxes on north-eastern coal landed at Billingsgate provided a reliable and vital source of funds for the rebuilding of the City. Huge sums were raised in this way for the resurrection of the churches, eighty-seven of which had been destroyed in the fire. New brickfields were dug, the mortar often mixed with ash from the ruins to produce the classic London 'stock'. Timber supplies began to arrive from Scandinavia, stone from Portland, Kentish rag, and Reigate stone hauled by ox-carts over the hills from Surrey to be stacked at Battersea for shipment up and down the river. By 1670 more than a dozen new churches were under construction,

*Many people escaped the Great Fire of 1666 by taking to the river. The fire spread slowly enough for those in danger to grab some belongings and make their escape. After the fire the well-to-do left the City and began to make their homes in the new West End.*

including St Mary-le-Bow in Cheapside, the bells of which chimed the nightly curfew for apprentices to be back from their frolics and the origin, it is generally believed, of the saying that a true cockney is a Londoner 'born within the sound of Bow bells'.

*The Great Fire of 1666 as seen by a German artist. It shows the fire swept westwards by the wind and Southwark on the south bank protected from the inferno by the river. Though a large part of the old city, including St Paul's Cathedral, was destroyed, a new London rose phoenix-like from the ashes with remarkable speed.*

Less than ten years after the fire most of the City's churches, the Guildhall, the livery companies' halls and thousands of homes had been rebuilt, the Thames carrying on its tides a huge quantity of materials and providing through the boatloads of taxed coal the money to transform a large part of London into a brand-new city. The rebuilding of St Paul's Cathedral, the single greatest enterprise, was delayed as 47,000 loads of rubbish were cleared away. Much of this would have provided valuable archaeological evidence had the City authorities taken an interest in it at the time. But funds were short, and rebuilding was the priority.

It was not until 1694 that the new Cathedral began to take shape, by which time it was receiving £18,000 a year from the coal tax which provided funds for the architect Wren's huge orders for building materials. These included more than 50,000 tons of Portland stone, for which the bill, including carriage by ship and cart, was over £80,000. Another 25,000 tons of stone from other quarries around the country for the masons to work came upriver, as well as all the lead and timber used in the building. Eventually completed in 1710, this is the same Cathedral we see today standing proud above the river – built at a time when there were no canals linking the City with the north or west of England, no railways, and only deeply rutted and poorly maintained roads over most of the country. The Thames was then truly the lifeblood of London. But one of the consequences of the fire was to hasten the movement of merchants and the wealthy out of the City to new estates built to the west.

The spread of the fire westwards had been checked beyond the western City wall at the Temple, but the wealthy families living in the palaces that lined the Strand were thrown into a panic. When the Earl of Clarendon went home to Worcester House in the Strand he found that his wife had 'caused all my goodes to be throwne into lighters for Twitnam [Twickenham] and into Cartes for my new house and other palaces'. By that time the Strand palaces were becoming unfashionable and some had already become government offices; but the panic of the Great Fire finally put an end to that Venetian-looking stretch of riverfront between the Temple and Charing Cross as a favoured aristocratic district, as the grand families moved into what would become the West End of London. With them went the tradespeople who provided them with their luxury goods.

By 1700 two Londons had formed on the north bank of the Thames – the City as trading and financial centre and Westminster, the political capital around which the landed gentry gathered. And yet the only bridge across the river connecting Westminster with the southern counties of Surrey, Kent, Sussex and Hampshire was the crowded and inconvenient Old London Bridge. In an effort to get the traffic to flow more freely on the bridge an order was made in 1722 that traffic coming into the City should keep to the west, and that going south to Southwark should keep to the east – for the first time in history the English 'keep left' rule of the road was established. But the lack of a river crossing, in particular from Westminster, was becoming a lively political issue. The only alternatives to London Bridge for those travelling by carriage were the horse ferries at Lambeth and Fulham. After the Great Fire London desperately needed a new bridge, but it was a long time coming.

# I I

# Westminster Bridge

M any a stroller with a literary turn of mind mutters to themselves as they step on to Westminster Bridge the first line of William Wordsworth's poem: 'Earth has not anything to show more fair . . .' The sonnet 'Upon Westminster Bridge' is one of his best known verses and was composed on 3 September 1802, a date commemorated in 2002 by a number of radio programmes and parodied by at least one latter-day poet who felt that earth certainly did have a great deal to show more fair than the view from Westminster Bridge. Wordsworth himself crossed the river here only fleetingly with his sister Dorothy en route to the coast and the ferry to Calais. This was not the present Westminster Bridge, but its forerunner. Wordsworth and his sister were able to get such a fine view of London in the early morning because they were high enough up on their carriage to see over the balustrades which spoiled the bridge as a vantage point for pedestrians.

> Earth has not anything to show more fair:
>   Dull would he be of soul who could pass by
>   A sight so touching in its majesty:
> This City now doth, like a garment, wear
> The beauty of the morning; silent, bare,
>   Ships, towers, domes, theatres, and temples lie
>   Open unto the fields, and to the sky;
> All bright and glittering in the smokeless air.

> Never did sun more beautifully steep
>> In his first splendour valley, rock, or hill;
> Ne'er saw I, never felt, a calm so deep!
>> The river glideth at his own sweet will:
> Dear God! the very houses seem asleep;
>> And all that mighty heart is lying still!

Wordsworth's sister, Dorothy, more prosaically jotted in her journal for 31 July, the day they actually crossed the river:

> It was a beautiful morning. The city, St Paul's, with the river, and a multitude of little boats, made a most beautiful sight as we crossed Westminster Bridge. The houses were not overhung by their cloud of smoke, and they were spread out endlessly, yet the sun shone so brightly, with such a fierce light; that there was something like the purity of one of nature's own grand spectacles.

The sensibilities of these two romantics from the wild Lake District in the north of England capture a moment in the extraordinary life of this bridge which was in 1802 just half a century old. Among Londoners it had long been a subject of wrangling and an engineering nightmare: sections collapsed even before the bridge was completed.

Old London Bridge had, over the centuries, been maintained largely by a fund administered by the Bridge House Trust which had benefited from many bequests as well as the rent of the houses and shops built on the bridge. But when, in the teeth of much opposition from vested interests in the City and Southwark, the decision was finally taken that London should have a new bridge upriver at Westminster it was not at all clear who would pay for it. The costs included not only the fees of surveyors and engineers and the expensive materials required, but the compensation payments that had to be made to those who complained that a road across the Thames would ruin their business.

The battle to get a bridge built at Westminster was rehearsed in 1726 when King George I defied the protests of the watermen and the City and gave the go-head for a wooden bridge to be built at Fulham. A company was set up with the power to raise £30,000 in £1 shares and its first task was to compensate the owners of the ferry rights which belonged to the Bishop of London and the Duchess of Marlborough. They then had to pay £62 a year to support the widows and children of poor watermen. From competing designs for the bridge a timber structure was chosen and put up remarkably speedily: the first pile was driven into the river bed in March 1729 and it was open to pedestrians on 14 November, the whole thing costing £23,000. On 22 November the Prince of Wales crossed the bridge in a carriage on his way to hunt in Richmond Park and a week later it was open to all road traffic. Those on foot paid a halfpenny toll, carriages 2s 6d, providing a healthy income. This wooden bridge lasted a century and a half when it was replaced by a sturdier iron and stone structure which is now known as Putney Bridge.

City interests were opposed to a bridge at Fulham, a long way to the west of London Bridge, but the threat of a bridge at Westminster was much closer to home and opposition was much more fierce. Even before Fulham Bridge was built, two petitions had been presented to Parliament in 1721 setting out the case for a crossing somewhere in the vicinity of Westminster. Naturally enough, the signatories included those whose estates lay in the counties south of the river, who joined forces with the principal landowners of Westminster to present their case. The existing horse ferries, they complained, were inadequate if not dangerous.

The Lambeth horse ferry was notorious. It was the only alternative to London Bridge for anyone travelling with a horse and carriage and provided a useful income for the Archbishops of Canterbury who collected the tolls. However, it sank more than once. In 1656 it went down with some of Oliver Cromwell's horses, and seven years later it sank again carrying some belongings to Lambeth Palace itself. The men who ran the ferry were invariably unpleasant, and in 1701 an order was made to fine them 2s 6d if they upset passengers with their 'immodest, obscene and lewd' language. The architect Nicholas Hawksmoor remarked of it, in 1726, at the time the campaign to replace the ferry with a bridge was at its height: 'There is no need to say anything of the Badness and Inconveniency of Lambeth Ferry since there is scarce anyone ignorant of it.' The ferry continued to run until replaced by a bridge in 1862. It is commemorated in the name of Horseferry Road, Westminster.

However, London was growing and congestion on London Bridge was chronic. The battle for a new river crossing was joined and went on for years as counter-petitions from Thamesside objectors set out every imaginable nuisance a bridge at Westminster would cause.

Southwark opposed it because it would take away its trade and plunge its inhabitants into poverty; those with businesses on London Bridge said they would be ruined; those living both below and above London Bridge said it would alter the tides and cause flooding; St Thomas's Hospital said that the lives of its patients would be threatened; others that it would cause the river to silt up and upriver boats would no longer come down to Queenhithe Market with their produce from the West Country; watermen would be destitute and their families would starve – the litany of opposition to the bridge was almost endless. As the debate dragged on into the 1730s the owners of Fulham Bridge added their concern that another crossing would ruin their finances unless the same tolls as theirs were charged.

Despite the weight of opposition, the case for a new bridge was finally accepted. It was an historic turning point in the relationship between London and its river, for what might be called the 'road lobby' emerged victorious and it was not long before the Thames was criss-crossed with bridges to the great advantage of horse-drawn vehicles and the great disadvantage of watermen and lightermen. In May 1736 an Act of Parliament giving the go-ahead for the bridge was passed on the grounds that it would 'be advantageous not only to the City of Westminster but to many other of His Majesty's subjects and to the Publick in general'. To arrive at a scheme for turning the proposal into a reality, 175 commissioners were appointed, among them many members of the aristocracy and the Archbishop of Canterbury, who was to be compensated for the loss of income from the Lambeth horse ferry.

The building of the bridge had a farcical beginning. Parliament decided it could raise £625,000 by running state lotteries. It was not a novel idea: state lotteries had a long history going back to Elizabethan days. Sometimes successful, they were more often failures: subject to charges of bribery and corruption, and the money raised short of what was needed. Imagining there would be great public enthusiasm for a flutter on London's new bridge, 125,000 lottery tickets were put on sale at £5 each. Dubbing the enterprise 'The Bridge of Fools', Henry Fielding alleged that all lotteries were corrupt and accused the Government of trying to fund public works by diverting the public interest away from the popular pastime of throwing dice. Of the total raised, no less than £525,000 was to be given away in prize money to 30,000 lucky winners, leaving just £100,000 for everything from buying the land needed for the bridge approaches to putting up the bridge itself. And yet there was no clamour to buy lottery tickets and after a year only £40,000 had been raised.

A new Act floated another lottery, this time to raise £700,000 with 70,000 £10 tickets and fewer prizes – just 7,000 ranging from £10,000 to £20. This again failed to raise the money needed and with work beginning on the bridge yet more lotteries were organized. In the end five lotteries were held between 1737 and 1741, at which point the Government, still short of the necessary funds, gave up and provided an annual grant to keep the works going.

The Commissioners who met in the Jerusalem Chamber at

Westminster were offered a number of designs for the new bridge, some of them entirely of wood, others a mixture of stone and wood, and one entirely of stone. At first a scheme for a wooden bridge on stone piers was accepted, but public opinion was against it – a river crossing in the heart of the greatest city on earth should be more substantial. In the end the Commissioners appointed as engineer a Frenchman, Charles Labelye, who had had a rather chequered career and was not well known to Londoners. From a French Huguenot family which had fled to Switzerland following the persecution of Protestants in the late seventeenth century, Labelye is said to have arrived in London at about twenty years of age speaking hardly a word of English. He then spent some time in Spain and returned to London in 1728, having somehow acquired knowledge as a surveyor and builder of ports.

A novel piece of machinery brought in by Labelye was the horse-powered pile-driving engine, invented by a clockmaker, James Vauloue. Three horses harnessed to the spindle of a giant cogwheel were driven around on a platform set out on the river. As the wheel turned it wound in a rope attached to a pile which was raised and then dropped into the river bed. This innovation saved a great deal of time, but construction work constantly ran into trouble. The Great Frost in the winter of 1739–40 brought work on the bridge to a standstill when the two central arches of Portland stone had been completed. When the river thawed in mid-February many of the piles that had been driven into the river bed were carried off and one of the caissons for an arch was badly damaged. At the time the Commissioners were still not sure if the bridge should be made of stone throughout, but that winter they decided that it would be and new orders were laid at the Portland quarries in Devon. Then in March 1740 the British Navy in search of men to impress began harassing the coasting vessels bringing the stone along the south coast and up the Thames.

Over the next decade all kinds of troubles attended the slow progress of the bridge building: barges coming upriver hit the arches, causing damage and in 1748 a pier sank, suggesting that Labelye's structure was fundamentally unsound. The Venetian landscape painter Canaletto presented in 1747 a panoramic view of the river at the time of the Lord Mayor's Show in which he painted the bridge as complete and topped with statues that were never put in place. It seemed at the time that only as an artist's impression would Westminster Bridge ever span the Thames. From the beginning the project was jinxed, and it looked as if the hazards of war and weather would confound the engineers.

*A view by Canaletto through an arch of Westminster Bridge when it was under construction in 1747. In the distance, around a long curve in the river to the right, St Paul's Cathedral rises above the City on the north bank. In the foreground is Lambeth on the south bank. Both the watermen seen on the river and the City merchants opposed the building of this new bridge, which broke the monopoly of Old London Bridge.*

By February 1750, however, it was nearing completion and some Londoners had already taken a hazardous trip across it when an earthquake rattled the Palace of Westminster. Another tremor followed in March and though there was widespread panic the bridge withstood it. Work was completed by the autumn and the bridge was finally opened on 18 November 1750 and lit at night by thirty-two oil lamps.

Opinions about the bridge were sharply divided. Was it a noble structure and a fitting monument to the centre of a great empire, as Labelye himself believed, or something of a structural mess? Its hump-backed shape was certainly not very suitable for horse-drawn vehicles and at various times, especially at night, it was deserted and regarded as a desolate place. Notoriously, the diarist and biographer of Johnson, James Boswell, took a prostitute on to the bridge and noted that he had 'performed manfully' in his 'armour' – a contraceptive sheath. In 1753 in response to a surveyor's report that there was 'a great want of proper places to piss in at the four corners of the Bridge', four stone 'pissing Basons' were installed.

Foreign visitors were often impressed, however. In his *Journeys of a German in England in 1782*, the pastor Carl Philip Moritz wrote:

> To cross over this bridge is in itself like making a miniature journey, so varied are the sights. In contrast with the round modern majestic cathedral of St Paul's on the right, there rises on the left the long medieval pile of Westminster Abbey with its enormous pointed roof. Down the Thames on the right can be seen Blackfriars Bridge, hardly less lovely than its neighbour upon which we ride . . . On the Thames itself pass back and forth a great swarm of little boats, each with a single mast and sail, in which people of all classes can be ferried across; and so the river is nearly as busy as a London street.

Little by little London streets were becoming busier, as the river was bypassed as a highway. Once Westminster Bridge was in place, the City of London gave up the struggle to prevent more river crossings and started building more bridges itself. The first of these was at Blackfriars, opened in 1769, and others were to follow so that the Thames in London was spanned several times upstream of London Bridge. Forced to abandon its bridge monopoly, the City widened the central arches of London Bridge in 1759 allowing the tides to run more fiercely under Westminster Bridge, the foundations of which proved early on to pose problems. In fact Labelye's old Westminster Bridge became something of a scandal with its need for constant repair: it survived for just over a century, when it was replaced by the present cast-iron bridge – officially opened in May 1862 without the hoped for attendance of Queen Victoria, then in her extended period of mourning for her husband Prince Albert.

# 12

# Wharves, warehouses
# and docks

~

Today you can take a very pleasant stroll around St Katherine's Dock just to the east of the Tower of London, cross the river by Tower Bridge and lose yourself on the South Bank among old warehouses with evocative names such as Butler's Wharf. In the past thirty years this part of London has been completely transformed and after a decade or so of dereliction is now a fashionable annexe of the City with expensive apartment blocks, museums and restaurants, most of which are smart and pricey. But when it was still a working part of the great port of London it was virtually out of bounds to all but a closely knit community of dockers, stevedores, watermen, warehousemen, clerks and tradesmen. The novelist Joseph Conrad, who spent years as a seaman before he began to write, first saw this stretch of the Thames when he sailed into London on *The Duke of Sutherland* in 1879.

It recalls a jungle by the confused, varied, and impenetrable aspect of the buildings that line the shore, not according to a planned purpose, but as sprung up by accident from scattered seeds . . . In other river ports it is not so. They lie open to their stream, with quays like broad clearings, with streets like avenues cut through thick timber for the convenience of trade. I am thinking now of river ports I have seen – of Antwerp, for instance, of Nantes or Bordeaux, or even old Rouen where the night watchmen of ships, elbows on rail, gaze at shop windows and brilliant cafés and see the audience go in and out of the Opera House. But London, the oldest and greatest of river ports, does not possess as much as a hundred yards of open quays upon its river front. Dark and impenetrable at night, like the face of a forest, is London's waterside.

The port of London had not always been like this. Before the rapid expansion of trade in the nineteenth century, which gave rise to a great wall of warehousing on both banks of the river below and above London Bridge and the excavation of a vast area of enclosed dockland to the east, the waterside was much less forbidding to outsiders. The landing of goods from abroad and the coastal trade took place below London Bridge; that of inland trade above it. In the Middle Ages the built-up area of the City did not extend far from the river and the sounds and smells of the Thames would have pervaded the lives of all its inhabitants. It was London's main highway and the very heart of its commerce. The loading and unloading of ships along the riverfront was part of everyday life.

The porters who pushed the carts and carried the cargoes to and from the ships had their own exclusive organizations. Merchants wanted reliable men and showed those they employed due respect. Porters had to vouch for their honesty with a surety and references from householders, and there arose several fraternities who specialized in particular lines of trade. From 1508 the Tacklehouse Porters employed by the Vintners Company had the sole right to handle imported wines, and they later extended their monopoly to carrying the wool imported by the Haberdashers from Spain as well as the merchandise of Grocers, Slaters and Fishmongers. By the eighteenth century the Tacklehouse Porters had the rights to the goods of the East India Company, all coastal trade, the South Sea Company, Ireland and British plantations. Working under them were the 'ticket' porters who handled goods from the Baltic as well as all pitch, tar, deal, flax and hemp. 'Fellowship' porters dealt with corn and other goods measured by 'dry weight'.

Merchants and porters lived close to each other and shared the same streets. Every year the ticket porters sent the families of merchants they worked for nosegays – little bouquets of flowers – to be worn at a special service in St Mary at Hill Church in Lovat Lane in the City. London was a seaport with stocks of rope, tar and all the other goods for keeping vessels shipshape stored in warehouses along the hithes and quays. Up until about 1700 roughly a quarter of the population is thought to have worked in one branch or another of the shipping industry. From then on London began to outgrow its port as housing was built further and further away from the river: the exodus of merchants after the Great Fire of 1666 had hastened the trend.

Throughout the eighteenth century the trade in London's port grew to supply the expanding city not only with exotic goods but with much of its building materials, food and fuel. Whereas around 1,200 sailing ships a year had moored in the Pool of London below Old London Bridge in the early 1700s, by 1794 there were 3,663 vessels coming up the Thames annually, at times so crammed together on the river that lightermen could not get their barges between them to unload their cargoes. Since the narrow arches of Old London Bridge made it impossible to extend the port upstream, the old port became chronically congested – with ship's captains frustrated by delays in selling their cargoes, merchants doing deals on the quays, and theft from ships left idling on the river a serious problem for merchants and shipowners alike.

Matters came to a head in 1796 when a committee of the House of Commons sat down to consider what needed to be done about 'river pirates' and the overloading of the port, which was not only crowded with ships but rapidly silting up. Members of Parliament learned about 'scuffle hunters' who stole goods from the quays, 'light horsemen', revenue officers and mates on ships who spirited goods away duty free, 'heavy horsemen', porters and labourers who concealed stolen goods in their baggy clothing, 'mud larks' who threw goods overboard and picked them up at low tide, and 'night plunderers' who cut barges free from their moorings and picked them up downstream. It was estimated that merchants were losing anywhere between £250,000 and £800,000 a year, many millions at today's prices.

The Commons committee looked at a number of schemes to make the port more efficient, but were frustrated by rival interests. Merchant companies wanted to be able to build new docks off the river with secure warehousing safe behind high walls. The porters and river quay owners protested that they would lose trade. Meanwhile a magistrate in Wapping, Patrick Colquhoun, wrote a report on crime on the river and suggested a temporary solution: a police force. Colquhoun, a Scotsman who worked in the cotton trade and had lived in Virginia in the United States, brought a fresh eye to the problems of the port and managed to overcome an entrenched English prejudice against 'policing' which was regarded at the time as an oppressive European institution. His river police, formed in 1798 with a magistrate, a clerk, a chief constable and a small band of men, was the first organized force in London, and indeed in the country. The Metropolitan Police Force was not formed until 1829.

Colquhoun persuaded the West India merchants that they could cut down on pilfering if they got their porters to wear stockings and breeches instead of their favoured baggy clothing. But this attempt to stamp out crime did nothing to ease the congestion in the Pool of London, and in the end the merchants won their case to create entirely new and more secure docks downstream. For this they had to push through new Acts of Parliament. The West India merchants, dealing in sugar and rum, were the first to get a scheme going. They chose a site a long way to the east of the old port on the Isle of Dogs (the name is probably derived from the Dutch *dijk* meaning dyke) which was undeveloped. Coming up the Thames their ships could leave the river by a lock gate before rounding the great loop by the Isle of Dogs. There the cargoes could be unloaded and stored in warehouses before being shipped out from the other side of the dock through a new canal which linked them with the river on the last stretch into London. It was a neat short cut across the north of the Isle of Dogs and the land, being undeveloped, was therefore cheap. Nevertheless it was anticipated that to make money the new dock company would need a monopoly on goods from the West Indies and this was granted for the first twenty-one years of its operation.

The West India Docks, where the giant tower blocks of Canary Wharf and bank headquarters now rise above the London skyline, were opened in 1802 and began a spate of dock-building which worked its way back towards the old Pool of London. These new docks, with high protective walls and guarded gates, became an entirely new and forbidding region of the city, and effectively put an end to the atmosphere of the old port. Although each new dock required an Act of Parliament the redevelopment was driven solely by commercial enterprise. A consortium of merchants and other City interests put up the money to cut out new docks in the old sailor town of Wapping. This was part of London's East End and compensation had to be paid for the loss of homes and businesses, as well as to Shadwell Waterworks which claimed that the dock would interfere with its pumping operations on the river. On 31 January 1805 these new London Docks were opened, again with a twenty-one year monopoly: all ships coming to London with tobacco, wine, rice and brandy (except that imported by the East India Company) had to unload their cargoes here for that period. Then in 1806 the East India Company opened its own docks at Blackwall, where for a long time it had had shipbuilding yards, and so another huge region of the Isle of Dogs was excavated for the unloading and storing of cargoes that had formerly been held in City warehouses.

The final annihilation of the old port came with the carving out of St Katherine's Dock on the eastern edge of the City. It took its name from the 700-year-old St Katherine's Hospital which was demolished in the development along with the homes of 11,300 riverside Londoners, most of whom were poor and were offered no compensation. They had to make do, moving

*A crowded quay in the West India Docks in 1840. Opened in 1802, these were the first of the new enclosed docks built by merchants to solve the problem of congestion on the river and the theft of cargoes. Huge office and apartment blocks now rise above this quay, while surviving warehouses have been converted into restaurants and cafés. A new Museum in Docklands has opened in part of the last surviving warehouse.*

into mean streets with names like Dark Entry, Cat's Hole, Shovel Alley and Pillory Lane. The developers of St Katherine's Dock planned the opening of their venture to coincide with the end of the monopolies on early docks, anticipating a bonanza when they could handle the unloading of a great range of goods right next to the City. However, St Katherine's Dock, built as it was in such a confined area, had to be smaller than the others and this hampered its operations as ships grew in size. The earth excavated for these docks, which were opened in 1828, was shipped upriver to be used as landfill for the marshy region where the great London builder Thomas Cubitt was creating the new stuccoed region of Belgravia.

Every new dock-building scheme was opposed by the watermen who in time found a way of undermining the economics of the dock companies. In the Acts passed for the building of the docks they persuaded Parliament to include a 'free water clause'. This, argued the watermen, was based on their age-old rights to the 'freedom of the river' − apprentices today still talk about 'getting their freedom' when they qualify. Dock water, so the logic went, was Thames water and watermen therefore had a right to take goods off the ships moored in the new docks and take them on to the river without the cargo ever going into a dock company warehouse. While the dock monopolies on specific goods lasted, the watermen's freedom was limited. But once these had expired they could take any of the goods straight from ship in the docks and deliver them to warehouses on the river.

In theory the new dockland would do away with the need for riverside warehouses, but because of the 'free water clause' they survived and new ones were built, served by the watermen who crowded the river with their motor-less lighters, 'driven' or steered with huge oars and propelled almost entirely by the tides. So London remained a river port but one which had grown away from the City and was built downstream of London Bridge where it became the 'forest' described by Joseph Conrad in 1879.

Among the sights of this crowded scene was the itinerant 'purl man' or beer seller, who plied his trade on the river among sailors, coal-whippers, watermen and lightermen. With a little fire on board to keep him warm, he rowed a broadly based skiff which could withstand the heavy swells created by the new steamers as they churned by. Henry Mayhew describes his trade in *London Labour and the London Poor*:

> Thus equipped he then goes to some of the small breweries, where he gets two 'pins' or small casks of beer . . . after this he furnishes himself with a quart or two of gin from some publican, which he carries in a tin vessel with a long neck, like a bottle – an iron or tin vessel to hold the fire, with holes drilled all round to admit the air and keep the fuel burning, and a huge bell, by no means the least important portion of his fit out . . . With this tin gin bottle close to his hand beneath the seat . . . and his fire pan secured on the bottom of his boat, and sending up black smoke he takes his seat early in the morning and pulls away from the shore, resting now and then on his oars, to ring the heavy bell that announces his approach. Those on board the vessels requiring refreshment, when they hear the bell, hail, 'Purl ahoy'.

As larger and larger ships came up the Thames new docks were built with wider lock gates and deep and wider expanses of water. Railway and canal companies promoted some of the new schemes such as the Victoria Docks, at that time the furthest east of any, opened in 1855 by Prince Albert. South of the river another consortium of interests, which included the Grand Surrey Canal Company, incorporated existing shipbuilding docks into a new dock scheme which came to specialize in corn and timber. The 'deal porters', whose skill was to heave on to their shoulders long, pliable pieces of timber and to half-run half-walk with them on runways of bouncing planks, became the characteristic workhorses of the Surrey Docks and did not disappear until the 1970s. So London's port spread south away from the City and ever eastwards until in 1866 the East and West India Dock Company created Tilbury Docks miles down the estuary in Essex. Tilbury was ahead of its time: in the first year of operation a line of German steamers from Central America were its only customers.

★

The whole of this vast area of dockland was created piecemeal by private enterprise, and cut-throat competition as well as the watermen's 'free water clause' undermined profitability. In an effort to reduce costs the new dock companies did away with the old fraternities of City porters, while concern at large-scale pilfering caused several to set up their own police forces, or even armed militia, to protect their cargoes. In time, dock labour itself became casualized – in demand only when ships arrived, when a huge and often desperate army of displaced Londoners would be drawn to dockland to queue for work, their hooks in one hand, the other raised to catch the attention of the foremen doling out the day's work. Wages were cut and the dockers, never well organized as trades unionists because of the uncertain nature of their work, finally struck in 1899 demanding what the newspapers called 'the docker's tanner' – six pence an hour. It was an extraordinary event, for the dockers enjoyed widespread public support and were backed by lightermen and stevedores (who packed cargo in ships) with two of the leading activists, Ben Tillett of the Wapping Tea Operatives Union and Will Thorne of the Gasworkers Union, not even dockers themselves. Some £24,000 is said to have been collected by the unions for the striking dock workers and their families from the public and from sympathetic City people, who blamed the month-long closure of the docks on the inefficient dock companies.

London's dockland was once again the subject of urgent government inquiry and in the end the entire network was nationalized. In 1909 the Port of London Authority, a public body, began the monumental task of modernizing the whole system, which still had men working cranes with treadmills, great wheels which they turned like hamsters in a cage. Only five years after the PLA came into existence, the threat to shipping on the east coast and in the Channel from the German Navy forced most trade on to the west coast of Britain. After the war, the PLA, with its headquarters in the City, did a great deal to

improve conditions in the docks, modernizing the 'Royals' –
Victoria and Albert Docks – and opening in 1921 the brand new
George V Dock. The trade handled by docklands continued to
grow until the outbreak of the Second World War when once
again shipping had to move to the west, and the docks themselves became a target for the Luftwaffe. In the Blitz the timber
in Surrey Docks became an inferno and many other docks were
badly damaged.

After the war there was a resumption of dock traffic on the river
but it had become a world apart from the rest of London, its sights
and smells familiar only to lightermen, stevedores and dockers.
Activity survived until the late 1960s and then, with almost unbe-
lievable speed, began to disappear. More and more goods were
packed in huge metal boxes – containers – and the old docks and
riverside wharves could not handle them. Nearly everything
shifted downriver to Tilbury and ports on the east coast. Some of
the cargo ships were now almost the size of medieval London
itself and the Thames could not carry them. One by one the inner
docks closed and the warehouses were abandoned, their loading
doors facing the river like eyes sealed in death.

For nearly twenty years what had been the greatest river port
in the world lay largely derelict, attracting a wonderful array of
wildlife. Plans were laid for its revival as an industrial region with
huge blocks of publicly owned housing, but they came to
nothing. Then in a bold and controversial move Margaret
Thatcher's Government, in 1981, created a new authority, the
Docklands Development Corporation, and offered any investors
prepared to risk their capital out on the Isle of Dogs a fantastic
deal – a chance to develop land free of planning controls and
commercial rates, with capital investments written off against
tax. Soon the tugs which once took sugar into the West India
Docks – the dockers called the sugar quay 'blood alley' because
their hands bled from the abrasion of the granules – were coming
up the Thames hauling barges filled with sand and gravel. They

turned in through the gates of the West India Docks carrying materials for the building of huge tower blocks, most of them, like Canary Wharf, funded by foreign investment.

The Isle of Dogs, which in 1802 had been a no man's land miles to the east of London, rose again as a glass and concrete extension of the City. Oliver's Wharf on the river, which had been packed with tea chests, was converted into flats and within a decade the river and dockland were transformed, the river almost emptied of its traffic, its shores a playground for architects who have enjoyed the freedom to design buildings unfettered by most of the constraints which confine their ambitions in 'historic' London.

You will see tugs towing huge barges stacked with brightly coloured containers and manoeuvring expertly between the arches of the bridges – up, as ever, on the flood tide, down on the ebb. They are carrying London's rubbish from two depots on the south bank above London Bridge down to huge landfill sites in Essex. A few smart little cargo boats lying low in the water, like the old coal-carrying flat-irons from the north-east, take sand upriver from Kent and Essex. Some of London's building material still comes up the river. But Conrad's dockland 'forest' has been cleared and people sail in the old docks where the big liners once called and live in apartments drinking tea where once, within living memory, the chests of their favourite brew were carried ashore by dockers.

Nowhere is the contrast between modern-day dockland and its vibrant past more poignant than the surviving quays of ' blood alley'. Mountainous tower blocks arise from the old West India Docks while converted 'dutch barges', some floating homes, others art galleries, are moored to the old stone quays built in 1802–3. Where the dockers once wielded their hooks and hoisted sacks are wide-open spaces on which restaurant umbrellas have been set out sheltering café tables and chairs. In the early evening the sound systems of the bars pulsate among the old brickwork and timbers of the surviving West India merchants' warehouses. Here the long awaited and beautifully laid out Museum in Docklands opened in the spring of 2003, taking revellers and tourists back in time to the colourful days when this was part of a working port such as Henry Mayhew described in the 1850s:

> As you enter the dock, the sight of the forest of masts in the distance, and the tall chimneys vomiting clouds of black smoke, and the many coloured flags flying in the air, has a most peculiar effect . . . The sailors are singing boisterous nigger songs from the Yankee ship just entering; the cooper is hammering at the casks on the quay; the chains of the cranes, loosed of their weights, rattle as they fly up again; the ropes splash in the water; some captain shouts his orders through his hands; a goat bleats from some ship in the basin; and empty casks roll along the stones with a heavy drum-like sound. Here the heavily laden ships are down far below the quay, and you descend to them by ladders; whilst in another basin they are high up out of the water, so that their green copper sheathing is almost level with the eye of the passenger; while above his head a long line of bowsprits stretches far over the quay; and from them hang spars and planks as a gangway to each ship.

# 13

# A view of the river

~

It is only very recently that Londoners and visitors to the capital have been able to get a panoramic view of the Thames and the great metropolis spreading around it without going up in a balloon, an airship, aeroplane or helicopter. There was no equivalent of Paris's Eiffel Tower and the public have no access to the tallest buildings. However as part of the Millennium celebrations in 2000, with many events on or near the river – the first time in half a century that the Thames had been the focus for a major celebration – an extraordinary structure appeared on the South Bank. It was delivered by river and very nearly ended up in it as it was being gingerly hoisted into position. Sponsored logically enough by an airline, the extraordinary Ferris wheel known variously as the Golden Eye, the London Eye or the Millennium Wheel carries passengers in glass capsules over 400 feet (135 metres) above the riverside. It moves at a snail's pace so the vista on all sides, which on a good day can stretch for twenty-five miles when the viewing capsule is at the top of the wheel, unfolds gently.

Unlike the Millennium Dome, which sits on the south bank of the river at Greenwich like a deflated circus tent, the London Eye has been a tremendous success, carrying 800 passengers a day, and has played its part in bringing back to the river something of its historic attraction as a place for fun and recreation which was all but lost in the Victorian era when the river functioned as highway, sewer and supplier of putrid drinking water. Because it is set right on the river – the architects who designed it say they stuck a pin in the map of London and positioned the Eye in the very centre of the metropolis – as the capsules inch upwards the Thames is in view east to west all the way to the top. And at the foot of the wheel is the region of riverside known as the South Bank with its theatres, cinemas, concert halls and art galleries. The old County Hall, once home of London's metropolitan government, now houses an hotel and – appropriately enough for its position on the river – an aquarium.

Though reviving as one of London's popular pleasure grounds, the Thames riverside of the present day has some way to go before it matches the exotic setting and entertainments of the eighteenth and early nineteenth centuries. It was to the south bank, across the river and away from the built-up area of London, that by tradition Londoners took a wherry and went for a day or a night out. The first of the pleasure gardens was in the area known as Vauxhall (a corruption of Foulkes Hall, the name of a country mansion). Laid out in Charles II's time, the New Spring Gardens were an attraction which Samuel Pepys among others enjoyed. As he noted in his diary for 28 May 1667:

> It is very pleasant and cheap going thither, for a man may go to spend what he will, or nothing, all is one – but to hear the nightingale and other birds, and here fiddles and there a harp, and here a jews trump, and here laughing, and there fine people walking, is mighty divertising.

The New Spring Gardens had a long life and at the height of their popularity in the late eighteenth century became known simply as Vauxhall, by which time there was an admission fee and many spectacular entertainments. It is said that when the nightingales and other birds began to disappear as London grew, men with a talent for imitating birdsong were hidden in the bushes at Vauxhall to sustain the rustic atmosphere. When Westminster Bridge was opened in 1750 the owner of the gardens, Jonathan Tyers, had a road built to Vauxhall and for the first time visitors arrived by coach rather than by river. A local Lambeth historian noted:

> on the first night of the entertainments beginning, so great was the novelty of visiting that delightful spot in a carriage, that the coaches reached from the gardens to beyond Lambeth Church, which is near a mile.

*Vauxhall, the most celebrated of London's eighteenth-century pleasure gardens, as seen in 1785 by the artist Thomas Rowlandson. Until Westminster Bridge was opened in 1750, Vauxhall was reached by wherry and even at this time a trip on the river was part of the night out for many.*

A speciality of Vauxhall were the fantastic fireworks displays which would have matched or even overshadowed the Thames-side pyrotechnics that marked the beginning of the new millennium on the night of 31 December 1999. Another Vauxhall attraction of the early nineteenth century were the antics of a tightrope walker who called herself Madame Saqui. She would climb a pole to a tightrope suspended at a slope, the highest point sixty feet in the air with no safety net below her, and with a stick to help her balance descend slowly, pirouetting all the way as fireworks exploded around her.

Vauxhall Gardens was still going strong in the 1830s, and was described by Alfred Thornton in his *Don Juan in London*, published in 1836:

> the gardens are beautiful and extensive, and contain a variety of walks, brilliantly illuminated with variegated coloured lamps and terminated with transparent paintings, the whole disposed with so much taste and effect, as to produce a sensation bordering on enchantment in the visitor . . . the wonderful aerial ascent of Mme Saqui from the most astonishing height, on a tight rope; an exhibition that again transports the spectator in imagination to fairy land, since the ease, grace and rapidity with which this lady descends, aided by the light of fireworks that encompass her, and still more by the darkness of the surrounding atmosphere, combine to give the appearance of flight of some celestial being.

In 1742 a rival to Vauxhall was opened on the north bank of the river close to where the Chelsea Hospital, home to the Chelsea Pensioners, now stands. It had been the home of Lord Ranelagh and was bought by theatrical impresarios from Drury Lane Theatre who turned it into a pleasure garden. It was an instant success, attracting the aristocracy to its huge Rotunda where meals were served and the London 'quality' could see and be seen. James Boswell, biographer of Samuel Johnson, went there many times for the company and to cheer himself up. On 4 May 1763 he had been traumatized by watching a hanging at Tyburn, but his spirits had returned a week later and he noted in his *London Journal* for 11 May:

> This day I dined at Dempster's. Then dressed and at seven went to Lord Eglinton's, and with Mrs Brown and Mrs Reid went in

his coach to Ranelagh. I felt a glow of delight entering again that
elegant place. This is an entertainment quite peculiar to London.
The noble Rotunda all surrounded with boxes to sit in and such
a profusion of well dressed people walking round is very fine. My
spirits were now better.

Around the walls of the Rotunda were forty-seven boxes for
refreshments, with doors at the back which led to the gardens.
Twenty-three chandeliers hung from the broad ceiling of the
dome which was at its base 150 feet across. For a while Ranelagh
stole Vauxhall's thunder but it closed much earlier. The Rotunda
was demolished in 1805 and the grounds were sold off. With the
rise of the music hall in the mid-nineteenth century Vauxhall
struggled to survive and when it closed in 1859 – the year after
the 'Great Stink' – the Thames riverside was no longer the attractive place it had been in Pepys's day, when he could hear nightingales sing to the violinists in the candlelit gardens. As the
atmosphere became more polluted, and gas lighting made brilliant interiors possible, all forms of London entertainment now
began to move indoors.

There was one other rival to Vauxhall which had a brief heyday
in the 1840s, a small part of which remains today as a picnic area
on the Thames in Chelsea. This was Cremorne, another magical
parkland which had begun life in the 1830s as a Stadium and was
converted into a popular pleasure garden in the 1840s. Like
Vauxhall, Cremorne attracted Londoners with firework displays,
music and dancing and special events. In 1861 a tightrope walker,
Madame Genevieve, crossed the Thames from Cremorne to the
south bank. Such innocent entertainment was not, however,
what made Cremorne popular in its last years.

The surgeon and social reformer William Acton paid a visit
which he described in the second edition of his *Prostitution,
Considered in its Moral, Social and Sanitary Aspects*, published in
1870:

As calico and merry respectability tailed off eastward by penny
steamers, the setting sun brought westward hansoms freighted
with demure immorality in silk and fine linen. By about ten
o'clock, age and innocence, of whom there had been much in
the place that day, had seemingly all retired, weary with a long
and paid for bill of amusements, leaving the massive elms, the
grass-plots, and the geranium-beds, the kiosks, temples, 'monster
platforms', and 'crystal circle' of Cremorne to flicker in the thousand gas-lights there for the gratification of the dancing public
only. On and around that platform waltzed, strolled, and fed
some thousand souls – perhaps seven hundred of them men of
the upper and middle class, the remainder prostitutes more or less
prononcées. I suppose that a hundred couples (partly old
acquaintances, partly improvised) were engaged in dancing and
other amusements, and the rest of the society, myself included,
circulated listlessly about the garden, and enjoyed in a grim kind
of way the selection from some favourite opera and the cool
night-breeze from the river.

Cremorne was closed down in 1877 after a vigorous campaign
by local residents who considered it a den of iniquity. Some
while later Lots Road power station was built on part of the site
and all that remains today is a small open space run by
Kensington and Chelsea Parks Department.

Most of the riverside in the London region was heavily indus-
trialized from the mid-nineteenth century until the Second
World War and was hardly suitable for recreation. One bizarre
venture was the creation in 1934 of an artificial beach on the
foreshore by the Tower of London with 1,500 tons of sand.
Tower beach was a great boon for poor children who could not
get a seaside holiday further down the coast at Clacton or
Margate and was crowded at low tide on sunny days. There were
lots of activities such as sandcastle competitions, and up to five
hundred children and their parents could cram on to the artificial
strand with Tower Bridge looming over them. The beach, which

was given royal approval by King George V who was very keen on recreation for the masses, was kept open until the outbreak of war and revived again in the 1950s. It was not finally closed until 1971 when public sensibility about the quality of water in the Thames – undoubtedly much better than in 1934 – became a concern.

Bomb damage during the Blitz flattened large areas of riverside, providing an opening after the war for its revival as a focus of pleasure and entertainment. During the war the Royal Society of Arts had discussed a plan to stage an event, when peace finally came, to match the Great Exhibition of 1851 which had been held in the Crystal Palace in Hyde Park. After much debate and despite doubts that a war-ravaged nation could stage such a show, the London County Council allotted twenty-seven bombed-out acres on the south bank close to its own headquarters at County Hall for the Festival of Britain. Its tone was futuristic: as the architect Hugh Casson put it when he recalled the Festival: 'We all had, I suppose, in a way rather naive views that England could be better and was going to be better – that the arts and architecture and music and healthy air and Jaeger underwear and all these things . . . were in fact the keys to some sort of vague Utopia.'

Opened on 3 May 1951 by King George VI, the Festival of Britain was, to the surprise of many, a great success, attracting more than eight million visitors in just five months. A temporary 'Bailey' bridge was slung across the river for the crowds coming from the north, and steamers were laid on to take visitors from the Festival site upriver to a funfair in Battersea Park. The first stage of the Royal Festival Hall was built for the exhibition (there were later additions in the 1960s) and this building is the only survivor of this celebration which marked the beginning of the end of post-war austerity. Much of the site fell into dereliction and became rough and ready car-parking space, but gradually the South Bank developed into the vibrant arts centre it is today, with the National Theatre, the Queen Elizabeth Concert Hall,

the National Film Theatre and the Hayward Gallery built alongside. In the Queen's Jubilee Year of 1977 the southern embankment was renovated as a pleasant promenade and now teems with
tourists throughout the year.

# 14

# Palaces of refuge

~

Throughout London's history, while the city clung to the Thames, riverside palaces were built, one or two of which survive though most have long since disappeared. Two still stand proud on the river and have a similar and unusual history. Although they look as if they must have been built as palaces, they were not: they were founded in the seventeenth century as 'hospitals', one for veteran sailors and the other for veteran soldiers. The Royal Chelsea Hospital was built to the design of Sir Christopher Wren between 1682 and 1690 to provide a home for war-weary soldiers who had no families to care for them. It was supposedly inspired by a similar institution in Paris which caught the imagination of Charles II who commissioned it. Miles downriver, the vista of the palatial buildings of Greenwich suggest royal grandeur on an epic scale: this was once the site of the old Greenwich Palace in which Henry VIII and his daughter Elizabeth I were born. However, the buildings that stand there today with their magnificent river frontage are much later, the largest part designed by Wren with Nicholas Hawksmoor as his assistant. Incorporating some early parts of a royal residence, they were constructed as a Royal Naval Hospital for retired and maimed sailors just a year or two after the completion of the Royal Chelsea Hospital for soldiers.

*The Royal Naval College, Greenwich, around 1850 when it was still a refuge for sailors, who were a familiar sight in the grounds, chewing tobacco or accepting a peck of snuff from visitors. Twenty years later, when the Jack Tar pensioners had become something of an embarrassment, Greenwich became the Royal Naval College. Many of the buildings are now part of Greenwich University.*

That these palaces on the Thames were inhabited by a few hundred superannuated fighting men has intrigued visitors to London for a long time. In his *History of Chelsea and its Environs* published in 1829, Norman Faulkner wrote:

It has often been remarked by foreigners that the charitable foundations in England were more fitted, by their grandeur and extent, for the residence of kings; while her palaces, by their external appearance, seemed better calculated for the reception of the needy and unfortunate. But surely they could not have paid a nation greater honour; and when we survey the noble fabrics at Chelsea and at Greenwich, we cannot but feel proud that we live in a country which constantly affords an asylum to the helpless wanderer – which relieves the wants of the needy and allays the suffering of the sick to an extent, and with a liberality, unknown throughout the rest of Europe.

In their charming *The Book of the Thames* published in 1859, Mr and Mrs Samuel Hall described the area around the Royal Naval Hospital:

> It is quite impossible not to observe that old Jack-tars have their favourite 'runs' about Greenwich; you meet the same wooden leg at a particular corner, and at the same hour, almost (fair weather or foul) every day in the year, the same old trio 'chaffing' and 'yarning' on the same bench; the same 'lot', with their pipes, of an afternoon in the park; their weather-beaten, broken-up faces, and their broken-up limbs, become your 'familiars'.

According to the Halls' account, a friend of theirs who lived in Greenwich always took with him a snuff canister and sometimes a roll of 'pigtail' (chewing tobacco) for the comfort of the sailors.

Ten years after this was written, the Royal Navy decided to close the hospital and provide retired tars with pensions which would allow them to live 'in the community'. In 1869 the pensioners were gone and in 1873 the buildings became the Royal Naval College. It is suggested in *Dickens's Dictionary of the Thames* (1890) that the sailors about Greenwich had become something of an embarrassment:

> When the Hospital was occupied by the pensioners it became one of the sights of London, and it is possible that a too liberal distribution of baksheesh on the part of the public may have had something to do with the deterioration which was observable in the manners and customs of the in-pensioners during the later days of its existence.

The Royal Naval College moved from Greenwich in 1998 and a lease on the whole site was taken over by the Greenwich Foundation. A large part of the buildings are now occupied by Greenwich University.

Astonishingly the Royal Chelsea Hospital remains very much as it did in the seventeenth century, home to several hundred Chelsea Pensioners who for ceremonial occasions wear their distinctive and anachronistic red coats. The Gardens are now the venue for the annual Chelsea Flower Show, the proceeds of which help to sustain this ancient institution which also receives annually a generous government grant.

# 15

# Salmon, smelt and
# the fisheries

~

There is a story told over and over again as if it were gospel truth that the River Thames was once so full of salmon that London apprentices rioted in protest against being served this luxury fish too often. Exactly the same story is told about other English rivers which became polluted in the nineteenth century and lost their annual run of Atlantic salmon. It is, in fact, a fiction which expresses a widespread anxiety about the destruction of the natural world. Diligent research into original sources has produced not a single incident of apprentices rioting over a surfeit of salmon, and all the evidence suggests that this magnificent silvery, pink-fleshed fish was highly prized and expensive at all periods in history and not the sort of fare that would be served to impecunious young workmen. There are records of salmon being brought down to London from Perth in Scotland as early as 1334.

But the Thames was a salmon river – by no means the best in the country but sufficiently well stocked to provide some Londoners with a livelihood. The season ran from March to September when the adult fish, after spending four years in the North Sea, returned to their spawning grounds in the shallows upriver. There were fisheries at Wandsworth, Battersea, Putney and Fulham. The Lord of the Manor at Chelsea had the fishing rights from Battersea to Lambeth. In the eighteenth century these fishing villages were still sending salmon to the London market and there is a record of Fulham catching 130 in a single day in 1776. There were some astonishing catches in the eighteenth century. In 1784 the *London Chronicle* carried this story on 13 April:

> A salmon which weighed near 30lb was taken off one of the starlings of London Bridge by two watermen, who saw it leap out of the water at low-water mark, and immediately put off in their boat.

There is a record too of a Thames salmon which measured from the eye to the fork of its tail four feet five inches, with a girth of two feet four inches, weighing over fifty pounds.

*A rich harvest of fish was still taken from the Thames when this scene of the river below the newly opened Vauxhall Bridge was painted in 1821. But the once abundant salmon had almost disappeared as more and more sewage was pumped into the river, and the fishing industry was on the wane. It never revived, though the Thames is now full of fish: more than a hundred species have been recorded in recent years.*

The Thames salmon fisheries survived until the early 1800s, though the spawning grounds were being rapidly destroyed by the building of locks upriver and the dredging of shingle banks to improve navigation. In 1812 a weir was built across the river at Teddington, Middlesex, which proved to be an almost impenetrable barrier for the salmon and today marks the official tidal limit of the Thames.

There were still annual salmon runs but the pollution of the river with sewage began to kill off the fish in the 1820s and the popularity of the water closet finally wiped them out altogether. Salmon need a high level of oxygen in river water in order to survive and this was all consumed by the myriad microbes which feed on excrement. By the time a Salmon Fisheries Commission took evidence in 1861 there were no signs of salmon at all and their rapid decline was documented by a fishing family called the Lovegroves who kept a record of their catches at Boulter's Lock, upriver, from 1794 to 1821. In 1801 the Lovegroves took sixty-one salmon; in 1812 only eighteen; in 1819 only five; none in 1820; and one in 1821. They took their last salmon in 1824.

Salmon were not, however, the principal Thames catch. Far more important were smelt – delicate little fish which, when fresh from the water, smell of cucumber. Like salmon they were seasonal, caught between March and May when the adults came up through London to breed. Able to live in both salt and fresh water – being euryhaline, to use the technical term – smelt migrate from the mouth of the estuary to fresher water where they lay their spawn. They grow to about ten inches in length and move in large shoals, so they could be pulled from the river in bucket loads. The City of London had most of the fishing rights on the river and there is a petition of 1798 which illustrates how popular these little fish were:

The season of the year being uncommonly forward, and in consequence, the Smelts which are seldom fit to take till the beginning of April, being now in the Thames in large quantities, several persons, deputed by the main body of Fishermen, applied to the Lord Mayor, to allow them to begin fishing for Smelts immediately in place of waiting till the 25<sup>th</sup> of March.

Along with smelt, whitebait and eels were caught in large numbers and the fisheries of the Thames were a serious commercial business until the early 1800s. As early as the fifteenth century City of London records carry reports of fishermen being prosecuted for using nets with a mesh smaller than was allowed, and bailiffs chasing unlicensed men with bows and arrows. Commercial fishermen used a wide range of techniques to snare saleable fish, many working in peterboats on the river. These vessels were about twenty-two feet long, sometimes with a sail, and had a well in which to keep the fish alive until they were sold at Billingsgate Market in the City. In his famous survey of 1850 Henry Mayhew described the children who sold fish on the streets, which were mostly little 'dabs' trawled from the river, fried in linseed or vegetable oil, died yellow with turmeric and sold in a paper wrap. This was one of the favourite snacks of the popular French chef Alexis Soyer in the 1830s when, after finishing work in his famous kitchens at the Reform Club in Pall Mall, he would take a stroll into Soho for a night's entertainment.

Most of the Thames fisheries had been destroyed by pollution before the Bazalgette sewage system was in place. In his *History of British Fishes*, published in 1859, William Yarrell wrote:

Formerly, the Thames from Wandsworth to Putney Bridge, and from thence upwards . . . to the bridge at Hammersmith produced an abundance of smelts, and from thirty to forty boats might then be seen working together, but very few are now to be taken, the state of the water, it is believed, preventing them from advancing so high up.

Anglers did still cast a line into the docks, which were protected by lock gates from the worst of the pollution, and in the early twentieth century they might take a chance anywhere on the river, for some fish and eels did survive. But the rapid growth of London between the wars and subsequent bomb damage returned the river to a putrid state so that by the 1950s it was deader than at any time in its recorded history.

There then unfolded an extraordinary story which continues to the present day. It is one of the least publicized, and yet most spectacularly successful, ecological triumphs of the twentieth century. In 1957 a fisheries expert at the Natural History Museum, Alwyne Wheeler, was asked by the London Natural History Society to conduct a survey of the river. He found no fish at all for a distance of forty-eight miles through the metropolitan reaches. There was practically no oxygen in the water, and only a few eels, which can travel over land as well as in the sea and in rivers, survived. In the mud were huge quantities of bloodworms which could live on a minimum of oxygen. (There was such an abundance of them that an industry had arisen digging them out at low tide to sell as aquarium food.)

Once again the killer was sewage. Between the wars London's built-up area had doubled with the building of semi-detached suburbia. The new 'Dunrovin' housing was served by hastily built and not very effective sewage treatment works and effluent was finding its way into the river. The bomb damage of the Blitz then punctured parts of the Victorian sewage system so that in the immediate post-war years the Thames became foul in almost all weather conditions. A concerted effort was made in the 1960s by the Port of London Authority and the London County Council to improve purification at sewage plants and cut down on industrial pollution. Alwyne Wheeler and others awaited the return of dissolved oxygen in the water which would bring back some of the fish, possibly even the salmon which had disappeared a century and a half before.

In March 1964 a new power station was being built on the north bank of the Thames estuary at West Thurrock. Like all the earlier power stations upstream, it would get its coal from the north-east of England delivered in collier ships and draw water from the river for use in the generator. Because the river water carried a good deal of debris which would damage the power station's machinery, it was filtered. In March 1964 an engineer noticed on the filter screens an odd-looking fish and sent it to the Natural History Museum. Wheeler identified it as a tadpole fish, unusual for the North Sea. The engineer was asked to keep any further finds and soon had a sand goby, a stickleback and a lampern. These inspired Alwyne Wheeler to conduct an eccentric survey: he contacted the power stations sited all along the Thames from the Ford car works at Dagenham up to Fulham and asked them to send him any fish they found on the filter screens. At the same time the London County Council held fishing competitions and one or two expeditions were made to net fish in the river.

The fish populations recovered with remarkable speed. Cucumber smelt returned; so too did flounder, another fish which comes upriver to spawn, and soon a range of freshwater fish were found in the very heart of London. By 1990 more than 100 species had been recorded, and at the time of writing the total has topped 120 with the return of lampreys, the rather unappetizing-looking, eel-like fish which – as everyone seems to know – put an end to an English king. Henry I, third surviving son of William the Conqueror, is reputed to have died in 1135 of a surfeit of this fish. Lampreys later went out of fashion and in the eighteenth century were being sold to Dutch fishermen as bait.

In November 1974 a salmon was found on the filter screens at West Thurrock power station, in poor condition but still alive. A prankster wrote to the newspapers to say he had taken it out of his freezer and thrown it in the river, and – such is the scepticism of Londoners about the health of their own river – he was believed. But the Thames Water Authority was sufficiently encouraged to restock the upper reaches of the river with salmon parr in the hope that they would migrate to the sea and return as adults to spawn. Salmon ladders were built to help them past the weirs and locks. By 1988 the salmon were running again, and in one year 300 were recorded at Molesey in the freshwater river. They are not yet self-sustaining, but it is remarkable that salmon should once again be running unseen past the Houses of Parliament.

You will not see Members of Parliament fishing from the Commons Terrace, however, nor will you see many anglers with rod and line in central London. There are few surviving stairs down to the river, the tides run strongly, and the metropolitan reaches of the Thames have a transient fish population. But in that murky brown water below you as you peer over the bridges there are plenty of fish, unlikely as it may seem. From time to time fishing competitions are held and the fisheries people from the Environment Agency catch samples of fish in the river right opposite the Palace of Westminster, casting their nets from a shingle bank which at low tide provides firm standing.

For the watermen on the Thames and the river authorities the cleaner water has presented a new problem. Barnacles have returned to eat away at wooden piers and seaweed is creeping up from the estuary. On the south bank below the Millennium Dome feathery topped reed beds of *fragmites australis* are becoming established as it self-seeds in the once polluted mud. All this is wonderful for wildlife; and cormorants, looking in flight like pterodactyls, regularly fly in skeins over St Paul's on fishing trips to the river – they, and other fish-eating birds such as the great crested grebe, providing competition for anglers.

# 16

# The fatal flush

Stretching away to the north, south, east and west of the Thames as it flows under Westminster Bridge are the offices, workshops, factories and homes of more than seven million Londoners all of whom will, several times a day, go to the toilet. When they pull the chain or press the lever of their WC there is a cascade of water and the effluent is washed away. Naturally enough there is not much concern about where it all goes: it is not their problem and they can rest assured that the sanitary arrangements for the metropolis have been taken care of. Few Londoners, and even fewer tourists, strolling along the Thames Embankment between Westminster and Blackfriars on a summer's evening have any idea that a fair amount of the sewage from north-west London is flowing seaward in a brick tunnel deep below them. It is part of the 'low level' sewer constructed in the 1860s to the design of Joseph Bazalgette, an engineer knighted for his work, which can be regarded as one of the greatest achievements of Victorian London, though nearly all of it is hidden from view.

If you lean over the Embankment wall and look down at the river it looks pretty mucky today, full of brown silt and littered with rubbish swept in on the tides. But imagine what it was like when, more or less where you are standing, all the sewage from the buildings to the north of you discharged their sewage into the river under your nose. That is what it was like in the 1850s before

Bazalgette's sewers were built, and it was the stench of the Thames as it swilled around Westminster that persuaded a reluctant Parliament in 1855 to create the Metropolitan Board of Works in order to tackle this and similar problems. It hardly bears thinking about now, but not only was the Thames a vast open sewer, commercial companies providing water for drinking, cooking and washing to London households drew their supplies directly from it.

*Passengers on an early Thames paddle-steamer get a riverside view of the monumental works of the new Embankment being constructed in 1864. Included in the brilliant design of Joseph Bazalgette were brick-lined sewage pipes which ran north and south of the river and carried sewage miles downstream, easing pollution on the river.*

The crisis of London's sewage had had one primary cause – the popularity of the flush toilet or water closet: an invention that had existed for two centuries before being commercially manufactured in the early 1800s to supply a rapidly growing demand. For a water closet to operate satisfactorily a pumped water supply is needed and a sewer which will take the effluent away. Large parts of London had neither. Since the Middle Ages Londoners had lived as people in the countryside did with cesspits below their homes. When these filled up, a fraternity of 'night soil' men with the disgusting task of removing the sewage emptied the pits and trundled the contents out to market gardens where it was used as manure. Inevitably, as the city grew, their task became more and more onerous.

Sewers were built and maintained by local commissioners but their purpose was not to get rid of sewage: they were essentially storm drains which channelled the run-off from streets into the river. Penalties were imposed for improper use, yet all kinds of horrible material found its way into them to be washed down to the river: dead rats and dogs along with butchers' bones and discarded food. With overflowing cesspits and clogged sewers conditions were already bad enough by the time Londoners began installing flush toilets with the only outlet for them the existing sewers which flushed their contents straight into the Thames.

At more or less the same time a new and terrible plague broke out sporadically in London: cholera. First identified in 1831 in Sunderland in the north-east of England by a surgeon who had recently returned from India, this new disease was long disputed by doctors who had no idea how the infection was transmitted. The most popular theory was that it was spread by 'miasma' or bad air. But the belief that it was related to the disgusting state of the water supply, the sewers and the Thames gradually gained ground and added urgency to the need to do something about London's sanitation.

The turning point came in the summer of 1858. In June the Thames, flowing far from sweetly past the House of Commons (recently rebuilt after a devastating fire in 1834) gave off a hideous, sickening gas – the 'Great Stink' as it became known. On 30 June, reported *The Times*, officers in the Commons were suddenly surprised by members of a committee rushing out of one of the rooms in the greatest haste and confusion . . . foremost among them being the Chancellor of the Exchequer [Benjamin Disraeli] who, with a mass of papers in one hand and his pocket handkerchief clutched in the other, and applied closely to his nose, with body half bent, hastened in dismay from the pestilential odour.

In the best tradition of the politics of 'Nimbyism' – 'not in my back yard' – Disraeli had, within two weeks of being evicted from a committee room by the river which he described as 'a Stygian pool reeking with ineffable and intolerable horrors', put in place all that was needed to provide London with its first systematic and comprehensive sewage system. The newly created Metropolitan Board of Works was charged with responsibility for commissioning the work.

Overseen by Bazalgette, this huge undertaking, which cost millions of pounds, involved the building of miles of brick sewers both north and south of the river and channelling effluent out to the east, to be discharged at Barking on the north bank and Crossness on the south bank, well away from the built-up areas of Victorian London. As far as possible the sewage was propelled by the dip of the land, but on the low-level sewer which runs under the Embankment pumping stations were required. The fine Victorian steam-driven station at Abbey Mills east of the City still stands as a monument to this enterprise.

Completed by 1865, the new sewage system cost £4 million and, with its three tiers of sewers running both north and south of the river, was capable of handling 420 million gallons of sewage and rainwater daily. In the House of Commons politicians breathed a sigh of relief as the Thames began to recover and fish returned. But that was not the end of the story: a century later the water quality in the river reached its nadir.

# 17

# The Thames on tap

~

Not long ago, a television documentary which questioned the claims of purity made by various brands of mineral water impishly included in a blind tasting at a supermarket a glass drawn straight from the tap. In the judgement of shoppers Thames water was placed in the top four, and subsequent scientific analysis confirmed that it was among the purest in terms of bacterial content. By contrast, one brand of 'spring water' was found to have several thousand times the permitted level of bacteria. Yet few people, whether Londoners or tourists, like the idea that when they fill the kettle or take a swig of water from the tap what they are getting comes from the murky, rubbish-strewn Thames they have seen swirling under the bridges in the centre of town. Today, of course, no drinking water is drawn from the river in London itself: it is syphoned off in the upper reaches and held in huge reservoirs where it is filtered before being pumped into the mains. However, for a very long time much of London's water came direct from the Thames, even in the period when the concentration of raw sewage had killed off the salmon in the river. It was pumped out by commercial companies which, despite mounting evidence to the contrary, were reluctant to admit there was anything un-savoury about it.

London once had plenty of good, clean water. When it was

still by modern standards a small town and the Rivers Fleet and Walbrook ran down from the country to the Thames, there were numerous springs in the gravel terraces north of the river. But by the thirteenth century a rising population, which brought greater demands for water while at the same time contaminating existing sources, was already causing problems. The City authorities were continually in search of new supplies 'for the good of the whole realm . . . to wit for the poor to drink and rich to dress their meat'. According to the sixteenth-century chronicler John Stow foreign merchants, most of whom were French, put up funds to lay a conduit or water-pipe from the River Tyburn to Cheapside in the City. Before the West End developed, the Tyburn, running along what is now Park Lane, was a clear stream beyond the built-up area of London.

For a while conduits seemed to be the answer, tapping off relatively unsullied springs and streams and piping them into the densely populated areas. The River Westbourne supplied Westminster, and Westminster Abbey leased springs at Paddington in 1439 for 'two peppercorns' a year; in 1471 the pipes were run as far as Fleet Street. The street name 'conduit' still survives in a number of places, such as Lamb's Conduit Street which was named after William Lamb who had the water pipe at Holborn relaid. There was a great deal of wastage from these water pipes, which were made from hollowed-out elm logs crudely slotted together. All the water was distributed by gravity and was provided free for householders who would collect it themselves on certain days. Only a few had the right to draw off the conduit water into wells in their homes by means of what were known as 'quills'. Commercial users such as tanners and brewers had to pay for supplies unless they had their own wells. There were annual celebrations at the spring heads at Paddington and Tyburn where dignitaries from the City would ritually test the water before hunting the hare in the countryside around.

However, such were the demands for water that it was also

collected from the Thames, though as early as 1297 the Earl of Lincoln had declared it unfit to drink because of the pollution from the tanneries. In the City there was a Company of Water Tankard Bearers who drew supplies from the river, despite the fact that this water was always full of silt and sometimes quite saline if the flow of fresh water from upriver was low. By the end of the sixteenth century London had come to rely more and more on supplies from the Thames. The first major commercial venture was a tidal mill built into the northernmost arch of Old London Bridge which drove a pump to draw water from the river. It was built by a Peter Morice (sometimes spelled Morris) who is variously described as a Dutchman or a German. London Bridge Waterworks, as it became known, began operations on Christmas Eve 1582. And to demonstrate the efficacy of his mill, Morice pumped a jet of water over the steeple of St Magnus the Martyr Church near by. With customers paying for their supplies, Morice's mill became a profitable business and in the course of time encouraged the establishment of others.

Though London Bridge Waterworks served as a major supplier to the City, its tidal mill had a limited range and new sources had to be found as the city spread northwards. For many years a scheme was discussed which would tap off water from springs in the countryside and descend by a carefully gauged series of channels aligned with the contours of the land to form an artificial river flowing into London. Work was finally begun in 1609, overseen by Hugh Myddelton, a City merchant adventurer and goldsmith; but after two years the project ran out of money. To complete what became known as the New River, King James I put up the remaining funds in return for half the profits. Taking water from springs in the villages of Chadwell and Amwell in Hertfordshire, and following a meandering course from the north into Islington, the New River fed into a reservoir in Clerkenwell and was officially put into operation in 1613. With its supplies distributed through leaky elm-log pipes the New

River Company was an important supplier of drinking water for many years. A windmill installed in 1709 pumped water to a second, higher reservoir near by, later to be replaced by a horse-driven mill and finally, in 1769, by a steam engine. Later the New River Company drew much of its water from the River Lea which ran into the Thames to the east, a connecting channel having been cut through Stoke Newington. Even so, water was rationed everywhere in London and the poor had to queue up at standpipes: there was no constant water supply as is taken for granted today – a situation that was by no means unusual or considered backward in the mid-eighteenth century.

In one of his evocative letters home the Frenchman César de Saussure wrote in 1725:

> One of the conveniences of London is that everyone can have an abundance of water. The big reservoir or cistern near Islington, the York Buildings Machinery near the Strand and that of the bridge supply every quarter abundantly. In every street there is a large principal pipe made of oak wood, and little leaden pipes carry water into all the houses. Every private individual may have one or two fountains in his house, according to his means, and pays so much a year for each – these fountains giving three hours' water in every twenty-four. Besides the pipes there are in many streets pumps and wells where poor people who cannot afford to pay for water can obtain it for nothing. Absolutely none is drunk. The lower classes, ever the pauper, do not know what it is to quench their thirst with water.

Although there were frequent complaints about the *quality* of London's water, especially that pumped from the Thames, in the eighteenth century it was the *quantity* that was regarded as the greatest problem. It seems that poorer Londoners at the time drank principally what was known as 'small beer' produced by breweries which generally drew their water from deep wells. There were street sellers of drinking water too, but they could hardly quench the thirst of the growing multitude as London continued to expand. Conduits provided no more than a trickle, the old wells were polluted and the rivers poisoned and gradually built over. From the mid-eighteenth century on, with London relying more and more on the Thames itself for its water supply, improved steam technology made it possible to pump increased supplies from the river.

As well as Morice's tidal watermill at London Bridge, the Shadwell Waterworks had been supplying the area of Limehouse and Whitechapel since 1669 by means of a horse-powered mechanism for raising the water into tanks. In 1750 an 'atmospheric engine' was installed, a forerunner of the steam engine, which could operate a simple pumping mechanism and had been developed to suck the water out of mines. By the late eighteenth century the greater efficiency of steam engines made it possible for more and more commercial companies to go into the business of selling Thames water to customers. It was a profitable business and led to fierce and often ridiculous and wasteful competition as rival companies laid down parallel sets of elm-log pipes in the same streets.

Long established and relatively primitive waterworks had been established on the Thames since the late seventeenth century – there was York Buildings Waterworks near Villiers Street just off the Strand as well as Shadwell and several others. But these were becoming outmoded by 1800 when the Thames water boom got under way, and new companies were established to supply districts on the ever-expanding edges of London: the South London Waterworks in 1805, the East London Waterworks in 1807, the West Middlesex Waterworks in 1806 and the Grand Junction Waterworks Company in 1811. Although these new companies began by offering supplies locally, with new steam engines and iron pipes replacing elm-log piping they found they could pump water into storage reservoirs and sell it over a wide area. Most drew their supplies from the Thames, though one of the largest and most successful was the East London Waterworks

Company which opened its Old Ford Works in 1809, pumping water from the River Lea. Despite its dubious source the company launched itself with a fanfare, installing a stand for spectators at the inaugural ceremony and providing music by the First Tower Hamlets Militia and Loyal Bow Volunteers, who played *Rule Britannia* and *God Save the King*. A sermon was read out on the theme of 'Thou shalt smite the rock, and there shall come water out of it, that people may drink'.

Discussion about the wholesomeness of the water being provided by the Thames companies makes strange reading now and in the light of subsequent epidemics. In 1805 Ralph Dodd, an engineer and promoter of waterworks, wrote:

> Thames water being kept in wooden vessels, after a few months, often becomes putrid . . . and produces a disagreeable smell. But even when drunk in this state, it never produces sickness; therefore it is evident no harm or ill occurs to persons whose resolution . . . induces them to drink it.

A widespread view was that once you had let the sediment settle in fresh, unfiltered Thames water it was fine – better, some said, than New River water.

In the 1830s, when the popularity of the flush toilet was swishing thousands of gallons of sewage into the Thames, the water companies were still drawing it out and selling it untreated. Households that bought supplies stored their water in tanks where it brewed horribly. In 1832 the first outbreak in London of Asiatic cholera took an estimated 5,300 lives in Rotherhithe, Southwark, Lambeth, Limehouse and Ratcliff and struck even in districts away from the river in Marylebone and Holborn. The realization that Londoners were drinking their own sewage gave rise to a chorus of complaints against the water companies. In 1850 an investigator, Arthur Hill Hassall, published *A Microscopic Examination of the Water Supplied to the Inhabitants of London and the Suburban Districts*. Collecting samples, Hassall reported of one experiment:

A gauze bag, tied to the top of the water cistern is found, at the end of a few days, to contain a mass sufficient to fill an eggshell, consisting principally of the hairs of mammalian animals.

Dead dogs, cats and rats as well as sewage found their way into the water supply and of the 'monster soup' served up in Southwark Hassall concluded:

This water was in the worst condition which it is possible to conceive any water to be, as regards animacular contents, in a worse state even than Thames water itself, as taken from the bed of the river.

*To supply the rapidly growing population of London with water, commercial companies pumped it straight from the Thames into wooden storage barrels where it festered. William Heath's satirical representation of water quality in 1828 is not too far-fetched. What he called 'Monster soup' was not banned until 1852 when supplies had to come from the cleaner stretches of the Thames, upriver of Teddington Weir. About 70 per cent of London's fresh water still comes from the Thames.*

There were reports by doctors which suggested that contaminated water might be the cause of cholera epidemics but in the
absence of any real understanding of microbiology there was no
proof. Following a virulent outbreak of the disease in 1849 a
London doctor, John Snow, published a work mapping its inci-
dence and relating it to the source of water supplies. Even this
classic epidemiological study failed to persuade the Victorians
that they were creating the ideal conditions for cholera to thrive.
Only the weight of official inquiries demonstrating the poor
quality of the water, irrespective of whether or not the Thames
was the source of the disease, finally induced the Government to
overhaul the system of water supply. In 1852 a Metropolis Water
Act was passed compelling companies which took supplies from
the Thames to shut down their old works and to source their
water from the river above Teddington Lock.

Since not all companies were obliged to comply immediately,
John Snow had a chance to compare the fate of the customers
of two companies, one supplying fresh, filtered water from
upriver and another still pumping straight from the Thames in
London. When cholera struck again in 1854 Snow found there
were more than 4,000 deaths among customers of the Vauxhall
Water Company, which tapped the Thames at Battersea,
whereas only 460 deaths occurred among customers of the
Lambeth Company which took its water from the upper
Thames. If that were not proof enough, Snow, with the help of
a young priest, traced an outbreak of cholera in London's Soho
to the pump in Broad (now Broadwick) Street and had it shut
down. The nappies of a baby who had died of a cholera-like
disease were washed in water that was then poured into a sink
that went into a cesspool which overflowed into the Broad
Street well. By shutting off the pump Snow famously averted an
epidemic. The parish authorities however soon had the pump
working again and discounted Snow's theory. It was not until
1883 that the organism which causes cholera was identified and

medical science finally accepted that Snow, by then long dead, had been right.

London began to get a recognizably modern water supply, with taps, washbasins and baths, from the 1870s and constant running water at the very end of the nineteenth century. In 1902 the commercial water companies were disbanded and a Metropolitan Water Board was established which began to create the large reservoirs to the west of London over which planes fly into Heathrow. From a window seat you can look down on those artificial lakes which today supply 75 per cent of London's drinking water: now distributed in a new ring main, it is judged to be as pure as that which runs from the taps in any major city.

# 18

## Freeing the bridges

~

You can stroll or drive over any of London's bridges today without putting your hand in your purse or pocket and paying a toll. The City of London kept London and Blackfriars bridges free, but private promoters of new crossings did not have the reserve funds and in order to raise income all, initially, made a charge for both pedestrians and horse-drawn vehicles. The first venture after the completion of Blackfriars Bridge was upriver between Battersea on the south side of the river and Chelsea to the north. The ferry which operated there was considered unreliable and hazardous and a local landowner, Earl Spencer (ancestor of the late Lady Diana Spencer), secured an Act of Parliament in 1766 to replace it with a bridge. Trying to raise money for a stone bridge, he offered for sale £1,000 shares which carried with them the right to vote in county elections; but when this scheme failed to raise the necessary funds, Earl Spencer settled instead for a timber bridge, which was opened in 1776 as Chelsea Bridge. A charge of one halfpenny was made for foot passengers and a scale of tolls set for horse-drawn vehicles, rising to a shilling for the largest. As a river crossing it worked reasonably well, but for river traffic the openings between the supports were too narrow and there were many accidents damaging both the bridge and shipping.

A spate of privately funded bridge building commenced in the early 1800s. A bridge to provide a route from Hyde Park Corner through to Greenwich, via Kennington south of the river, was begun in 1811 but redesigned before it had been completed. It was to have been of stone but the company promoting it ran out of money and switched to a cheaper design of iron arches on a stone base. This, the first iron bridge across the Thames, was opened in June 1816 with tolls of a penny for pedestrians and up to one shilling and sixpence for carriages. Originally called the Regent's Bridge, it was later renamed Vauxhall Bridge and, like all London bridges, was rebuilt at a later period.

While work on this bridge was going on, another enterprise funded by the Strand Bridge Company planned a crossing from Somerset House on the north bank to Watermen's Stairs on the Lambeth side. Five thousand £100 shares were issued for the project and a further £60,000 borrowed on the security of toll receipts. Faced in granite from Wales and designed by John Rennie it was opened in 1817, just a year after Vauxhall Bridge. It was to have been called the Strand Bridge but was renamed the Waterloo in honour of the Duke of Wellington's defeat of Napoleon two years earlier. Again the toll revenues did not give the investors in the bridge any return.

Less than two years after the completion of Waterloo Bridge a private company sought to profit by building a new crossing between Blackfriars Bridge and London Bridge. There were fierce objections from the City and the watermen as the river was now becoming crowded with bridges which were making navigation much more difficult. But a design by the engineer John Rennie which would leap the river and provide the minimum obstruction for shipping won the day and Parliament approved the plan. Rennie, a Scotsman, looked north of the border for the stone for the abutments and shipped granite blocks down from Peterhead on the east coast, as well as from Dundee and Edinburgh. Huge iron castings were made in Rotherham, Lancashire, and the girders winched into place and bolted together. This new crossing, Southwark Bridge, was opened officially when St Paul's struck midnight on the 24 March 1819. Why the promoters of this bridge ever thought they could make a profit is a mystery, for either side of them were City Corporation bridges – Blackfriars and London Bridge – which were toll free. So hard up was the company when it first began to take its toll money – nearly all of it from pedestrians – that it refused to pay Rennie his fees and expenses. Although he got most of his money after protesting vociferously, Southwark Bridge never paid its way and was notable for its lack of traffic while London (rebuilt to Rennie's design in 1832) and Blackfriars Bridges became more and more crowded.

As more bridges were built, south London began to develop, attracting more traffic, which put further pressure on the road system and created a demand for more river crossings. After 1830 the railways arriving from north, south, east and west were bringing in more passenger and goods traffic, all of which had to be hauled ponderously in horse-drawn vehicles across the town. By the 1860s congestion had become a serious problem. Private companies continued in their belief that they could profit from new river crossings, and in 1862 Lambeth Bridge was opened. But because of its steep approach and a general belief that it was unsafe it was not favoured by goods vehicles and, like Southwark Bridge before it, took most of its paltry income from commuters walking from the southern suburbs to work.

The Albert Bridge Company began work on yet another crossing in 1864 but it ran into trouble as a new Embankment was being built and Parliament dithered over its exact positioning. This company, in order to push through parliamentary permission for a new bridge, had offered to buy the wavering old Battersea Bridge once its own had opened and in the meantime to pay for repairs. Work on the Albert Bridge was delayed for nearly a decade and it did not open until 1873, by which time the company promoting it was more or less insolvent and could not recoup its cost with toll charges.

Though they never returned much in profits, toll charges did limit the use of bridges: toll gates narrowed the entrances, payments slowed down traffic, and the cost discouraged movement across the river. The first to recognize this was the City and in 1849 they leased Southwark Bridge from the company that had built it and made it toll free. In 1866 they bought it outright. Whereas the City has a long-established system of local government, the greater London that had grown up around it had no such central authority until the creation of the Metropolitan Board of Works in 1855. Formed initially to build the sewers, it took on also the task of improving the roads. Recognizing the problems of the toll bridges it decided to buy them up and remove all charges. Under an Act of 1877, it spent £1,400,000 to 'free' eleven bridges. To celebrate the event the Prince and Princess of Wales criss-crossed the river on Queen Victoria's birthday, 24 May 1879, in a carriage which took them over Lambeth, Vauxhall, Chelsea, Albert and Battersea bridges.

In the end private enterprise, as so often in London's history, was bailed out by the public purse. However, those who lived downriver of London Bridge and had contributed their rates (or local taxes) to freeing the river crossings in town argued that they had been hard done by. The solution was to provide a free ferry at Woolwich for both vehicles and pedestrians who were taken across the river in paddle steamers. Opened in 1889 the ferry still runs – on diesel – and remains a quaint and amusing way of crossing the Thames. Every one of the bridges acquired by the Metropolitan Board of Works was later replaced: the lifespan of river crossings on the tidal Thames has mostly been short, with the notable exception of Old London Bridge.

> Southwark: rebuilt/reopened 1921.
> Blackfriars: rebuilt/reopened 1869.
> Waterloo: rebuilt 1939–45.
> Westminster: 1862 bridge intact.

Lambeth:   rebuilt/reopened 1932.
Vauxhall:   rebuilt/reopened 1906.
Chelsea:   rebuilt/reopened 1937.
Albert:   bridge strengthened 1973.
Battersea:   rebuilt/reopened 1890.
Wandsworth:   rebuilt/reopened 1940.
Putney:   rebuilt/reopened 1886.

# 19

# The Boat Race

~

You might still today hear a Londoner refer to someone having an ugly (or just possibly a handsome) 'boat race'. In their choice of a slang rhyme for 'face' the cockneys lit upon an event which was arguably the first major national sporting event in England, the annual rowing race between crews from the Universities of Oxford and Cambridge which became a regular event on the Thames from 1856. Popular interest in the annual contest between crews from England's two most venerable universities eclipsed all other rowing competitions, even though the mass of London's population had no social or academic affiliation to either of them and probably a hazy notion of where they were.

There had been many races for watermen on both the tidal and the upriver Thames since the eighteenth century (Doggett's Coat and Badge race was just one). Betting was always a great attraction at any kind of contest and these races drew crowds who gambled on the outcome. And there was prize money or a valuable cup for the winner. In his *History of the Watermen's Company* Henry Humpherus describes a contest in which seven watermen rowed an evening race one May from Whitehall to Putney for a cup worth twenty-five guineas. Humpherus says:

> A great number of the nobility and gentry appeared in barges elegantly decorated with pennants, streamers etc., and rowed by

> watermen in handsome uniforms; their Royal Highnesses and
> . . . [a] band of musicians, were rowed in a barge ahead of the
> wagermen.

Betting and prize money were all part of the excitement and rowing races were sponsored by wealthy patrons. In the eighteenth century West End clubs, Boodle's and White's among them, sold tickets to their members for a place on livery company barges to follow a race from Westminster Bridge down to London Bridge and back, with a prize of ten guineas going to the winning team of young watermen. A supper would then be held at Ranelagh Gardens. One of the reasons for these races was to encourage the skills and strength of watermen who still provided so much of London's passenger transport. There was no concept of the 'amateur' as opposed to the professional rower, and nearly all the races were rowed on the river in London.

The origin of the Oxford versus Cambridge boat race was very different. Boating on the upper Thames became a popular pastime among university students and the leisured classes in the early 1800s. The river then was still used by a great deal of commercial traffic and the scope for pleasure boating was limited. Amateur rowers would hire their boats from watermen and sometimes row against them with dispiriting results: however fit a college student might be, he was unlikely to stand a chance against a skilled and seasoned professional. Watermen thought nothing of ramming their opponent to gain advantage or knocking away their oars, practices which were known as 'fouling'. Very soon, in order to enjoy a dignified competition which they had a chance of winning, young gentlemen declared that there should be 'no hired watermen' in their races. An amateur was someone who rowed for the fun of it and wanted (and probably needed) no prize money.

It was upriver at Henley that the first Oxford versus Cambridge boat race was staged in 1829. Surprisingly it attracted a crowd of 20,000 to the little riverside town, which sent by boat to London timber, meal and malt on heavily loaded barges. Noting the crowds that were attracted to the contests between the two old university teams, Henley held a public meeting in 1839 at which a resolution was passed:

> That from the lively interest which has been manifested at the various boat races which have taken place on the Henley Reach during the last few years, and the great influx of visitors on such occasions, this meeting is of the opinion that the establishing of an annual regatta . . . would not only be productive of the most beneficial results to the town of Henley but . . . a source of amusement and gratification to the neighbourhood, and to the public in general.

At the very first Grand Challenge Cup staged in May 1839, which was to establish Henley as a leading attraction of the London 'Season', the contestants were confined to college students from Oxford, Cambridge or London universities, Eton or Westminster School, officers of the two brigades of Household Troops, or any other club which had been in existence for a year. The implication was that no watermen were invited to compete, but the concept of the 'amateur' had yet to be defined. It was not until the 1870s that the issue of who could row at Henley came to a head with the first teams arriving from North America. In 1878 this included a crew of French Canadian lumberjacks who entered for the Steward's Cup and alarmed the Henley officials by shouting battle cries as they stormed up Henley Reach.

From then on only amateurs were permitted to take part, meaning those who had never competed for money; had never competed against a professional for a prize; had never had anything to do with teaching or engaged in any 'athletic exercise' for a living; had never been employed 'in or about boats'; and who had never earned a living as a mechanic, artisan or labourer. It did not matter if the crew members wanted no money and were prepared to abide by the rules of the race: they had to be gentlemen. The Henley 'amateur' rule was later adopted by the Metropolitan Rowing Association which became the Amateur Rowing Association. Nobody could be an amateur rower if they had ever been 'engaged in a menial duty'. Keen rowers who had worked as plumbers or bricklayers were left to found their own associations and in 1890 they set up the National Amateur Rowing Association, allowing in anyone who did not compete for money or work on the river.

*London's first great sporting event, the Oxford and Cambridge Boat Race rowed on the tidal Thames from Putney to Mortlake, drew huge crowds to the riverside. This is a lithograph of the crowd watching the event in 1871 when there was a great deal of gambling on the outcome. The 'Light Blues', Cambridge, won by a boat length.*

The snobbery of oarsmen on the Thames extended into other sports such as cricket, football, rugby and tennis and was not discarded from some of them until the late twentieth century. It is all the more surprising that the Oxford and Cambridge boat race should have become such a hugely popular public event in

London. It was first rowed in the metropolitan reaches in 1836 between Westminster and Putney, but there was too much commercial shipping for safety and in 1845 the route was moved upriver. The teams then began to hammer out some rules. Oxford objected to Cambridge having as a coxswain a waterman who was not above a bit of 'fouling' if his oarsmen were in trouble, and in 1846 a resolution was passed to the effect that a coxswain ought to be 'a thinking, reasoning being in a higher degree than any watermen have shown themselves to be'.

By 1856 the 'Battle of the Blues' (called after the colours the individual teams sported) had settled down to a regular, orderly event in which most of London and much of the country took an interest, declaring themselves to be either for Cambridge or Oxford on an entirely arbitrary basis, unless it was for colour preference or they had laid a wager on a team. In 1881 the *Illustrated London News* reported:

> The popular mind of London yearly gets into a fit of more or less affected excitement upon the favourite occasion that comes off on Friday morning, as usual, along the famous rowing course of the Thames from Putney to Mortlake . . . It is not a little remarkable that the declaration of zealous sympathetic partisanship for one or other of these learned and revered academical corporations, the two ancient English Universities, should be most frequently uttered by the mouths of babes and sucklings, of servant-maids, errand boys, and the illiterate streetocracy, who can have no possible reason for partiality to either serene abode of classical studies. 'Are you Oxford or Cambridge?' these simple folk demand of everyone they meet, as if it were a contested election when one is supposed to be Liberal or Tory.

It was like that in London at least until the 1950s, and though the intense excitement which once packed the riverside and bridges with spectators and drew huge television coverage has waned, the Boat Race still attracts an audience worldwide of some eight million viewers.

## 20

## Railways

~

Canal building in the late eighteenth and early nineteenth centuries had linked the River Thames with the industrial areas to the north of London and to farming regions to the west and south. The era of 'railway mania' which began in the 1840s not only increased road traffic in the capital, it established an entirely new network of routes into London which took no notice of the River Thames. Some of the early locomotives were shipped on the river – the *North Star*, destined for Isambard Brunel's Great Western Railway, was built in Newcastle and brought down to the London Docks, then taken by barge to Maidenhead. Some locomotives arrived on the canals. But once the lines were laid there was little need for river transport, and the Thames had assisted in its own demise as a highway between London and the upriver towns.

In the 1853 edition of *Jackson's Oxford Journal* the Reverend Vaughan Thomas wrote a series of letters which chronicled the commercial decline of the river to the west of London:

> Trade, prosperous trade, may be said to have taken flight from the District, and may now be seen in the heavy-goods train, whirling eastwards at the rate of twelve to fourteen miles an hour, whistling in derision as it passes by the Thames and Canal navigations, and by its speed mocking the drowsy barge (that emblem of the old slowness of traders and the torpid course of their com-

mercial transactions) which would reach the rail train's terminus in four or five days and nights after it, and then return in eight or ten days more, if it escaped being grounded in the passage home.

The railways knocked out the trade of the non-tidal river above Teddington Lock and freed it for rowing races and pleasure boats. They also made the dreamy reaches of the Thames beyond Maidenhead much more accessible to the leisured classes who travelled out to Henley for the Royal Regatta. In 1902 a total of twenty-six trains was laid on to take the gentry from Paddington to a branch line at Henley on Brunel's Great Western Railway. An army of extra staff was drafted in, signals were changed and goods wagons carrying coal, ballast and chalk were held back. Jerome K. Jerome's classic comedy about messing about on the river, *Three Men in a Boat*, has his fictional characters taking the train from London and persuading the driver to alter his route for their convenience.

Railways running west could outpace the river. But for those companies linking the south and the Continent with London, the Thames presented a formidable barrier. A new spate of bridge building to carry trains across the river began with the opening of the Grosvenor Bridge at Victoria in June 1860, to carry the London and Chatham Railway. On the north side of the river an entirely new fashionable region of 'wedding cake' stuccoed housing had been built in Belgravia and Pimlico for just the sort of people who might hop on a train to the Channel ports en route to their favourite summer resorts at Deauville or Honfleur or their winter watering holes on the Côte d'Azur. The London Brighton & South Coast Railway Company and its subsidiary, the Victoria Station & Pimlico Company, bought a disused basin of the Grosvenor Canal and got permission to span the river with what became known as the Victoria Bridge. With funds from other railway companies this second bridge was built in 1865, followed by a third in 1907.

All along the Thames in central London railway bridges ran alongside the existing road bridges until the watermen and lightermen heading up on the tides from the docks might have thought they were driving their barges through a tunnel. Each new bridge created a novel set of currents as the river swept through the arches, and each new generation of watermen had to learn how the river 'set' as they steered their way through.

*The first railway bridge across the Thames opened in 1860, bringing steam trains from the south into Pimlico, leading, in time, to the building of Victoria Station.*

However, one unintended consequence of the arrival of railways was the enormous increase in the demand for carthorses, which in turn created new demands on river trade. Until the early years of the twentieth century nearly all transport on London's roads was horse drawn. The new railway lines brought in not only passengers but millions of tons of produce that had to be unloaded and delivered in wagons and carriages of various kinds. A wonderful little book published in 1893 called *The Horse-World of London*, by W. J. Gordon, has chapters on the Cab Horse, the

Carrier's Horse, the Post Office Horse, the Vestry Horse, the Brewer's Horse, the Queen's Horse, the Jobmaster's Horse, the Coal Horse, the Cavalry Horse and the Omnibus Horse. The 'fuel' for this transport system was hay and oats, which were in as much demand then as petrol is today. Indeed, with London in the late nineteenth century requiring about a million horses to keep it going, there were periodic 'hay crises' at times of poor harvest.

In most years, however, feed for London's transport came up the Thames in red-sailed barges piled high with hay and known as 'stackies'. These sailing barges were designed for local estuary and south coast work, river lorries which could be handled by a man, a boy and a dog. Flat bottomed and broad beamed, they could sail into shallow water and creep into the creeks along the Essex and Kent coasts to pick up hay from local farms. A number of these sailing barges were owned by consortia of farmers.

In many paintings of the river in the nineteenth century these stackies can be seen tacking up past the Houses of Parliament, just clearing the bridges. In fact a bail of hay was sometimes hung from below a bridge to indicate the clearance at an oncoming tide. When they had delivered their hay the bargemen loaded up with manure from the huge stables that were kept by railway companies, brewers and others: the new British Library is built on the site of a multi-storey horse-park that served St Pancras Station. The sailing barges took the manure back to the farms where it was spread to grow another year's supply of fuel for London transport.

The sailing barges had evolved from simple vessels built first in the late eighteenth century which, as they were made larger and more robust, took on work around the east and south coasts of England carrying grain, bricks, building materials and other goods from the agricultural regions of the Thames estuary. After the Second World War many were fitted with diesel engines and were still at work in the 1970s. Thereafter most of the barges were left to rot or were broken up, but one or two have survived and have been restored to take tourists and boating enthusiasts out on the river.

# 21

# Tower Bridge

~

You could be forgiven for believing that the intention behind the bizarre appearance of Tower Bridge was that it should become one of the few instantly recognizable monuments of London and a huge tourist attraction. It looks like no other Thames crossing and has no counterpart on any of the great rivers of the world. And it is true that its mock antiquity, achieved with stone cladding on an iron frame, is purely decorative. The unusual structure of Tower Bridge was for the most part entirely practical, however, for it was built at a time when there was still tremendous competition between road and river traffic in London. In its first years the two central bascules would be raised majestically by hydraulic power fifty times in a single day to allow ships through on their way to and from the coast. Shipping had right of way and the horse-drawn carts and carriages had to wait as steamers and sailing vessels cruised by on the tide.

When it was officially opened on 30 June 1894 Tower Bridge represented an ingenious solution to a serious problem in the

*The scene on Tower Bridge not long after its opening in 1894. As well as allowing ships to pass upriver when its bascules were raised, the roadway of the bridge was laid flat which made it easier for horse-drawn buses and carts with heavy loads to cross.*

Pool of London immediately below London Bridge. A new road across the river was needed to cope with the amount of traffic going to and from the docks on both banks of the Thames, but it had to allow for the fact that some of the ships coming into the Pool of London were still tall-masted square riggers. A number of proposals for high, single-span bridges were put forward but they would have taken up too much land for the approach roads. A severely hump-backed bridge would have been a serious obstacle to traffic, for all vehicles were horse drawn and nobody anticipated that the motor car would be anything other than a novelty. Tower Bridge could allow the tallest ships through and ran flat across the river for horse-drawn road traffic. Pedestrians could take a lift to the higher level above the bascules and walk across even while a ship was going through.

It was an expensive solution with huge running costs. To be always ready to open for ships coming in on the tides it had to be manned for twenty-four hours a day. In the first years a superintendent and bridge-master were in charge of a crew of eighty: they stoked the coal-fired boilers which powered the hydraulic lifting system, kept all the machinery in good order, and supervised the traffic on the road and the river. In case any traffic became stuck on the bridge when a ship was going through a team of rescue horses was kept at the ready.

Only a few years after the opening of Tower Bridge, however, the tallest ships disappeared as steam finally replaced sail, and the first motor cars and then motor buses appeared on the streets of London. Over the years the bridge crew became depleted as fewer and fewer ships sounded their horns for the bascules to open and Tower Bridge became something of a costly white elephant. But removing it was unthinkable – though there were proposals to take it down – and the Bridge House Trust funds of the City which had been used to build it paid for the electrification of the lifting mechanism and it can now be operated by one person with the press of a button. Ships have to give twenty-four hours' notice if they want it opened and for most of the day it remains just a road bridge like any other in London.

It is still exciting to cross Tower Bridge and there is always that slight frisson of anxiety that the bascules might start to rise when your car or bus is halfway over: this actually happened in 1952 when a red double-decker full of passengers was caught mid-bridge and just managed to make it across. Today with the bridge-raising mechanism modernized and computerized the bascules are raised about 900 times a year. When liners come through in the summer to moor next to HMS *Belfast*, the cruiser which is a permanent feature just above the bridge, and sailing barges with their tall masts take tourists upriver, the bascules are sometimes raised up to twelve times a day. But road traffic now has right of way.

The pedestrian walkway over the top of the bridge was never popular. Rather than take one of the lifts to 400 feet above the river or climb the stairs, most people on foot preferred to wait for a ship to go through before crossing on the road. In 1910, being so little used, the walkway was closed; but it is now open again and incorporates a charming museum of the bridge. It is also a wonderful place to view the river looking east and west. Tower Bridge is no longer the river crossing closest to the sea. A long way downriver at Dartford, the Queen Elizabeth II suspension bridge, opened in 1991, flies high above the Thames to relieve the congestion in the Dartford Tunnel that was constructed in the 1950s.

## 22

# Walking across (and under) the river

~

One of the great sights of London in the morning and again in the evening is the steady flow of people striding across the Thames on their way to and from work. By tradition the tide of commuters runs south to north in the morning and back south in the evening and this is certainly still true of the bridges which cross the Thames into the City, for the Square Mile has a small resident population of only 7,000 while some 320,000 people are said to trudge in and out to work every day. Commuters crossing the river here are well served by the four bridges which the City itself maintains: Tower, Southwark, Blackfriars and London Bridge itself. To the west, upriver, the crossings are not so close together and for those on foot it can be a tiresome hike to one or other of the road bridges. However in recent years, with the watermen and their wherries long gone and only a scattering of ships on the river, it has been possible for the first time in many years to bridge the river for pedestrians.

One of the strangest tales in the history of Thames crossings was the construction in 1845 of a suspension bridge for pedestrians between Lambeth on the south bank and Hungerford Market which stood more or less where Charing Cross Station stands now. There had been a market on the site since the seventeenth century and in the mid-Victorian period it sold fruit, meat and vegetables. Designed by Isambard Brunel, the new bridge was only 14 feet wide but 1,440 feet long with a timber walkway held up by two massive cast-iron chains on either side running from Italianate towers. At either end were large abutments which provided piers for the steamers which were then plying the river with trippers and commuters. So Hungerford Market was not only linked by the bridge to the densely populated Lambeth bank but could be easily reached by river.

Exceptionally for a London bridge Hungerford made a profit, with 10,000 commuters a day paying the halfpenny toll. But it did not last long. Hungerford Market burned down in 1854 and in a few years the company which had built and run the bridge sold out to the railways. Brunel meanwhile was trying to finish his most famous work, the Clifton Suspension Bridge over the River Severn from England to Wales. He died in 1859 before the work was complete, but in his honour a memorial committee found £5,000 to buy the chains of his Thames footbridge and incorporate them into Clifton Bridge, which was finished in 1864. In the same year the South Eastern Railway's bridge, incorporating bits of Brunel's original Hungerford Bridge, was opened and the footbridge was retained. Pedestrians still paid a toll to cross until 5 October 1878 when the Metropolitan Board of Works paid the railway company compensation of £98,540 to abolish the charge as part of its 'free the bridges' campaign.

Hidden beneath the girders of the railway bridge this footbridge remained the only one of its kind in central London until the end of the twentieth century. Downriver of London Bridge there was no question of spanning the river for pedestrians or horse-drawn vehicles – river traffic was much too heavy – though as London grew in the nineteenth century the demand for a crossing became urgent. As early as 1798 a company had been formed to dig a tunnel further downriver between Gravesend and Tilbury, but the technical problems defeated them and the attempt was abandoned in 1802. Cornish mining engineers tried at the same time to use their specialist skills to create between

Rotherhithe on the south and Limehouse in the north a tunnel for 'Horses and Cattle, without carriages, and Foot Passengers'. The engineer Robert Vazie, known as 'The Mole', was joined by the Cornish giant, wrestler and engineer Robert Trevithick, inventor of the first steam-powered road vehicle and an early railway pioneer, and together they began to dig beneath the river. But they had miscalculated and after a thousand feet the tunnel caved in, very nearly drowning Trevithick.

The next attempt was begun in 1824 by Marc Isambard Brunel, father of the more famous Isambard Kingdom Brunel who built Hungerford suspension bridge. Brunel senior often spent time down at the Naval Dockyard in Deptford: his first great invention had been machines for mass-producing tackle blocks for the British Navy. A deadly little mollusc called *teredo navalis* was playing havoc with the ships' timbers as it bored neat little holes in the wood. Brunel senior, according to legend, always carried a magnifying glass, and he took a close look at the burrowing techniques of this pest. It had two sharp shells which it used to slice through the wood which it chewed, digested and then excreted at the back to form a kind of cement tunnel. This inspired Brunel to invent a giant version of *teredo navalis* for boring through the soft clay subsoil of the Thames Valley. Called his 'Great Shield', it was a large rectangular iron cylinder which was forced bit by bit through the ground with workmen bricking up the sides of the tunnel as it inched forward. With this he hoped to burrow under the river.

In 1824 a Thames Tunnel Company was formed and raised £150,000 on the promise of 'Great Publick Advantage if a Tunnel for the Passage of Carriages, Cattle and Passengers were made from some part of the Parish of St John Wapping to some part of the Parish of St Mary Rotherhithe'. Parliament, approving the scheme, allowed seven years for it to be bored out and set tolls of twopence for pedestrians and a scale up to two shillings and sixpence for carriages drawn by six or more horses.

Work began on the south side of the river in 1825 with an iron hoop 50ft in diameter and weighing 25 tons. Church bells were rung and the Thames Tunnel project was under way.

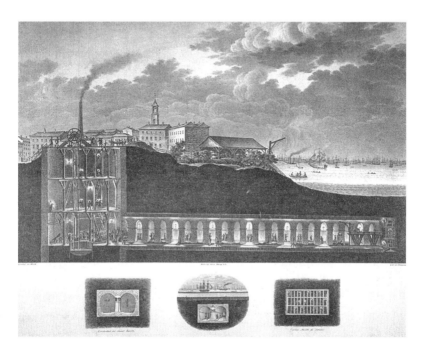

*A German illustration of the immense and hazardous labour involved in cutting the first tunnel under the Thames. Work began south of the river at Rotherhithe in 1825 but did not reach Wapping on the north bank until fifteen years later. The brainchild of Marc Brunel (father of Isambard Kingdom Brunel), the Thames Tunnel was not opened until 1843.*

The 'Great Shield' worked, but the subsoil was not consistently the malleable clay that Brunel had wished for and they hit sand and gravel which washed into the machine parts and held up the work. A huge labour force of 450 men forcing the shield forward, bricking in the back of the tunnel and pumping out water drained the company's resources. In 1827 a flood tide rushed into the tunnel through a breach and washed 120 men back to shore; miraculously, all of them survived. When the tide ran out the river was low enough for the breach to be sealed. But the trouble was not over: Brunel senior became ill from overwork and in time

*When it first opened, the Thames Tunnel attracted huge crowds. It was wide enough for carriages, but no approach roads were built and it was open to pedestrians only. Toll money paid by those wanting to walk under the river never covered costs and it became in the 1860s a railway tunnel, as it remains today on the East London line.*

his son Isambard took over. More than eighteen years were required to complete the tunnel by which time the newspapers were dubbing it 'The Great Bore'. The Thames Tunnel finally opened with a fanfare on Saturday 25 March 1843 when 10,000

Londoners paid to take a look at it. Later Queen Victoria and Prince Albert were rowed downriver in the state barge to inspect this wonder and in the first year more than two million people handed over their toll money to experience the delights of the Brunels' tunnel.

Although it was wide enough for horse-drawn vehicles, the company could not afford the cost of building suitable approach roads and the tunnel remained a pedestrian crossing. It became a popular tourist attraction and 'grand fancy fairs' were held in it with a variety of stalls, weight-lifting competitions and glass-blowing demonstrations. But none of this gave the directors a return on their money and the tunnel went into social decline, a favourite haunt of prostitutes. It was sold in 1862 to the East London Railway and trains began to run through it in 1870. The only way to go through it today is on the underground's East London Line between Wapping and Rotherhithe.

Twenty years before Tower Bridge was opened, a second Thames tunnel had been bored between Tower Hill in the north and Tooley Street on the south bank. An adaptation of Brunel's 'Great Shield' had been developed by the bridge engineer Peter William Barlow, using a cylindrical cutter and cast-iron rather than brick linings. With this more efficient burrowing device a Tower Subway Company planned to create a kind of prototype tube train, a fourteen-seater carriage hauled through the tunnel on a pulley system. The cutter worked well, burrowing under the river at the rate of ten feet a day, so that in just five months the tunnel was complete. First class tickets on the Tower Subway were twopence and second class one penny and passengers were promised rapid transit under the river in just two minutes. But the machinery frequently broke down and was eventually removed, leaving the tunnel as a walkway. It was little used and was closed in 1897, and now carries cables of various kinds. Commenting on its value as a walkway *Dickens's Dictionary of the Thames* for 1890 noted:

there is not much headroom left, and it is not advisable for any but the very briefest of Her Majesty's lieges to attempt the passage in high-heeled boots, or in a hat to which he attaches any particular value. It has, however, one admirable quality, that of having cost remarkably little in construction.

Despite these disappointments, there was a kind of burrowing mania in the last two decades of the nineteenth century as engineers and private promoters sought to find a way of linking the dockland regions north and south of the river below London Bridge. As with bridge building, most private enterprise schemes ran into financial trouble. It was the Metropolitan Board of Works which, in its last days, finally got a successful tunnelling scheme going. The brainchild of their celebrated engineer Joseph Bazalgette, designer of the sewage system and several bridges, it was planned on a route between Blackwall on the north bank and Greenwich to the south. Bazalgette did not see it through, however, for a new authority, the London County Council, took over from the Metropolitan Board of Works in 1889 and a new engineer, Alexander Binnie, was appointed. He brought in an American specialist firm, S. Pearson & Son, whose engineer E.W. Moir had just finished a tunnel under the Hudson in New York.

The art of tunnelling was becoming more sophisticated as new versions of the cutting shield were devised and compressed air was pumped in to maintain atmospheric pressure. The Blackwall Tunnel was designed with a carriageway for horse-drawn vehicles and two footpaths for pedestrians. It was opened on 22 May 1897 and within a year more than four million foot passsengers had used it and road traffic was counted at over 300,000 horse-drawn carts and carriages. This proved to be, as it still is, the main road route across the Thames between Tower Bridge and the Dartford Tunnel and the Queen Elizabeth II Bridge. A second tunnel was cut in the 1960s to cope with the increase in traffic, by which time the horses for which the tunnel was built had disappeared.

Several years before the Blackwall Tunnel was opened the new London County Council had wanted to get a ferry service going between Rotherhithe and Ratcliff to ease the flow of traffic between the southern and northern docks. This scheme was abandoned on the grounds that the ferries would be a hazard to shipping; instead, once Blackwall had opened successfully, a tunnel scheme was pushed through. This was the Rotherhithe Tunnel in which a narrow roadway was flanked by two footpaths. It was opened by the Prince of Wales, the future King George V, on 12 June 1908.

There was still opposition to these river crossings even in the late nineteenth century and when the London County Council proposed in 1896 that a tunnel for pedestrians should be built between Poplar and Greenwich there were protests from watermen, the London and Blackwall Railway and even the trustees of Greenwich Hospital, which owned Greenwich Pier. To push the scheme through, the LCC had to pay out a total of £30,000 in compensation to watermen and other river interests for lost business. With lifts on both banks the Greenwich foot tunnel opened in 1902 and was well used. Although there is a quicker way under the river since the extension of the Docklands Light Railway to Greenwich in November 1999, the foot tunnel, now a listed building, is still popular and is especially useful for cyclists who cannot use the railway.

Yet another foot tunnel was opened in 1912 between the terminals of the Woolwich Free Ferry because of complaints that the boats were constantly being held up by the London fogs, which descended every year before the Clean Air Act of 1956 took effect. The Woolwich Subway, too, was built by the LCC and is still open. With the redevelopment of Docklands since the 1980s these easterly river crossings are likely to become much more popular than in the days when the area languished in dereliction after the closure of the docks.

In central London no new river crossings had been built for a century when, in May 2000, Her Majesty the Queen inaugurated the strikingly original Millennium Footbridge which links St Paul's Cathedral with the Tate Modern art gallery, spanning the Thames and more than three centuries of history. An unanticipated structural problem, which made the bridge vibrate alarmingly under the footfalls of many pedestrians, led to the closure of the bridge for more than a year. It was reopened to the public in February 2002 and has proved to be extremely popular, especially with tourists who can get fine, traffic-free views of the Thames.

Hard on the heels of the Millennium Bridge, two new footbridges have been built along the route of Brunel's original Hungerford Market crossing. Work on these was delayed by the fear that there might be unexploded bombs from the Second World War in the river bed – the Luftwaffe had made a frequent target of the Hungerford railway bridge during the Blitz. Moreover, at this point the Thames was so riddled with underground railway tunnels that it was feared these might be breached when the pilings were sunk. Happily there have been no explosions and no terrifying punctures of tube tunnels, and the latest walkways across the river are now open.

# 23

# Cruising down the river

~

It is still possible to go back in time and take a steamboat trip on the Thames, for in recent years one or two of the old coal-fired boats have been rescued and restored. They are hired out by parties on a daily basis, smaller Edwardian boats starting out from the upper river whilst the larger paddle-steamers which occasionally visit from the Clyde in Scotland and other parts of Britain moor by Tower Bridge. Most Thames trips now, however, are taken on modern river 'liners' (as the owners like to call them) and last a few hours. It is worth taking a look at London from the river if only to get a better sense of its history, to feel the force of its tides and to appreciate the treacherous nature of the Thames and the skills of watermen who take you through its bridges.

There have been few serious accidents on the Thames, even when the river was crowded with wherries, lighters, tugs, sailing barges and steamers, and despite the many conflicts between watermen, records show that sinkings and fatal collisions were a rarity. It was therefore especially shocking when news broke on the night of 20 August 1989 that many young party-goers had been drowned when the Thames cruiser *Marchioness* was rammed in darkness by the much larger freighter, the *Bowbelle*, as it headed downriver on the ebb tide. Of the fifty-one who died many were trapped in the boat as it went down while others who dived into the river were caught in its fierce currents and were drowned.

This disaster, for which nobody has yet been held responsible, was a gruesome reminder of the power of the river. Frogmen searching for bodies asked for the Thames Barrier at Woolwich to be closed to give them some 'still water', and for four hours the tide was held back in London. Among the bereaved families a campaign continues to establish the cause of the collision and many new safety regulations have been introduced for Thames shipping. The *Marchioness* went down close to Southwark Cathedral which now has a memorial to those who died.

In the last decades of the nineteenth century day trips down the Thames on steamers became very popular: they would call at Gravesend, Sheerness, Southend-on-Sea, Margate and other coastal resorts. So that these large boats could take on passengers even at low tide piers were built, one of the longest at Southend: so long in fact that part of the fun was taking a little train along the pier to the boat. In London a popular starting point was Swan Pier by London Bridge and it was from here that the *Princess Alice* set out on a fine morning on 3 September 1878 heading downriver to Sheerness. It was by all accounts a jolly day out. On the return trip the steamer called at Gravesend and then headed out into the river with the band playing the topical music-hall song (Russia being the enemy at the time): 'We don't want to fight you, / But by jingo if we do, / We've got the ships, we've got the men / And got the money too.' It was evening and some women on the *Princess Alice* struck up a hymn, the crew intervened in a fight between a man and his wife, and children scampered about the decks. Just out of Gravesend, the steamer stopped and there was a sense that something was wrong. The trippers saw looming out of the dusk the lights of another ship and then felt the force of a huge impact.

A collier ship, the *Bywell Castle*, had rammed the *Princess Alice* which immediately took on water and began to list, throwing hundreds of trippers into the river eleven miles below London Bridge. It was said that many died because of the pollution in the water, though most would have drowned anyway. For days after the disaster bodies were washed up on the tides and when they were finally counted the death toll of 640 made this the worst disaster ever in British inland waters.

*One of the early Thames paddle-steamers calling at Gravesend in Kent in the 1820s. The pier built out into the Thames estuary allowed popular pleasure boats to dock even when the tide was out.*

Steamers continued to ply the Thames well into the twentieth century and even after the Second World War it was possible to board a boat at Tower Pier and go all the way to the east and south coast resorts. Those who are frustrated today by delays on trains and at airports might give a thought to the hapless steamer passengers who, travelling to their holiday resort at Clacton or Margate, sometimes found the seas so rough they were unable to land. If the bad weather had set in they would be brought all the way back to London to be put on a train.

# 24

# The river police

~

While the shrill wailing of police sirens is heard all too frequently on London streets, the launches of the river patrols rarely hit the throttle to attend an accident or to pursue a criminal. It is a measure of the commercial decline of the Thames that whereas it was once a hotbed of crime it is now a huge area of the metropolis in which fights and thefts are relatively rare. The Marine Police Force, founded in 1798 – some thirty years before the shore-based metropolitan force of which it now forms a small part – was funded at the start by the West India merchants and the Planters Company at an annual cost of £5,000. This paid for the lease of a building on the foreshore at Wapping and a small force of four 'surveyors' who manned rowing boats on the river with a Superintendent of Ship Constables in charge, and a larger body of thirty 'quay guards' with their own superintendent.

When the cargo docks were built they had their own policing systems but the Marine Police Force continued to patrol the river and were absorbed by the Metropolitan Police Force ten years after it was first established in 1829 by Robert Peel (from whom London policemen get the name 'bobbies'). Afterwards known as the Thames Division of the Met, the river police retained their headquarters at Wapping with its view over the Pool of London. It grew considerably in size in the nineteenth century: *Dickens's*

*Dictionary of the Thames* put the force in 1890 at 49 inspectors, 4 sergeants and 147 constables. A few detectives had joined the force in the 1870s but the number of arrests and convictions was rapidly declining as crime shifted away from the river. The Thames Division had also become speedier: by the 1880s it had its own steam launches and in 1910 its first motor boats, though rowing boats were still in use in 1925.

Though crime declined on the river, one gruesome aspect of police work has remained constant: the recovery of bodies from the Thames. In Victorian times the police were in competition with the scavengers who nightly trawled the river for corpses which might still have in their clothing money or valuables. Today the Thames Division – now renamed the Marine Support Unit – retrieves between eighty and a hundred bodies a year from the river and takes them to the Wapping Station for identification. It is thought that the great majority of those drowned have committed suicide by jumping off one of the bridges.

As the river has become cleaner and quieter it is used more and more by pleasure craft, and the Marine Support Unit spends much of its time getting amateur navigators out of trouble and rescuing them from the river. It also keeps a watch out for drug smugglers and terrorists and has two rapid-response inflatable dinghies and an Underwater Search Unit of volunteer frogmen. The river police were called in at the time of the sinking of the *Marchioness* in 1989, but the long series of investigations that followed argued strongly for a lifeboat service on the Thames. In February 2002 a London Coastguard unit was established with crews stationed permanently at Tower Pier, Chiswick Pier and Gravesend and volunteer crews at Teddington. Run jointly by the Royal National Lifeboat Institution and HM Coastguard and in constant touch with the Met's Marine Support Unit, the London Coastguard's 'search and rescue' boats cover a 55-mile stretch of the Thames. The expectation is that one of the rescue teams can be on the scene of a potential disaster within fifteen minutes.

# 25

# A strong brown God

London is built in the wide, shallow valley of the Thames and a large part of it lies within the natural flood plain of the river. Left to its own devices, the Thames would swamp all of Westminster and Whitehall, the Strand, much of the City, the South Bank and a very large swathe of new housing which has been built east of Tower Bridge as part of the renovation of the docklands. A few years ago the environmental pressure group Friends of the Earth produced a map to frighten Londoners into taking action to stop global warming. It showed the potential for disaster posed by a rise in sea levels of just a few feet. But Londoners do not live in fear of a great flood and tend to forget that without constant vigilance their lives would be as precarious as those of people whose city is built on a fault line which might shift at any time and shake buildings to the ground. Tens of thousands of commuters go to work each day in offices below the river's high water mark.

Global warming – whatever its true cause – is not regarded as the greatest threat by the government agencies concerned with protecting London from flooding. Far more significant are the weather conditions in the North Sea which can drive a wall of water down the east coast of Britain into the Thames estuary and all the way upriver to the west of London. At the same time, heavy rainfall within the Thames Valley can fill the tributaries of the river and send a surge of fresh water downstream to meet the oncoming tide. These are not new threats to London brought about by climate change, but age old. The *Anglo-Saxon Chronicle* records for the year 1099 that 'on the festival of St Martin the sea flood sprang up to such a height and did so much harm as no man remembered that it did before.' Stow's *Chronicles of England* gives this account of a thirteenth-century flood:

> In the year 1236 the River Thames, overflowing its banks, caused the marshes all about Woolwich to be all a sea wherein boats and other vessels were carried by the stream, so that besides cattle a great number of inhabitants there were drowned, and in the great Palace of Westminster men did row with wherries in the midst of the Hall. Moreover in the year 1242, the Thames, overflowing the banks about Lamberhithe [Lambeth] drowned houses and fields by the space of six miles, so that in the Great Hall at Westminster men took their horses, because the water ran overall.

Samuel Pepys described in his diaries a great flood on 7 December 1663 when all Whitehall was 'drowned'. These very high tides were exceptional but devastating when they happened, and London has lived for centuries in the knowledge that to protect its buildings it has had to put up higher and higher flood defences. In doing so the river has gradually been hemmed in so that tidal surges push further inland. Decade by decade the exceptional tides have got higher and higher because the Thames Valley and London itself have been sinking seaward while sea levels have risen.

When the Victorian embankments were being built between 1869 and 1874 an estimate was made of the highest possible tides. The Metropolitan Board of Works ordered the owners of riverside properties to have defensive walls 17 feet 6 inches high. This was sufficient to hold back tidal surges in 1874 and 1875. But not everyone complied with the regulations and in 1881 the Thames rose to the Board's height limit and overflowed its banks. On 18 January 1881 *The Times* reported:

> Yesterday a calamitous high tide occurred on the Thames, flooding, in addition to many other places, the low-lying neighbourhoods between Blackfriars and Westminster Bridges. The most heart-rending scenes were witnessed . . . The most damage was done to houses lying between Upper Ground Street and Waterloo, many buildings being flooded with five and a half feet of water . . . ice floes piled on the Speaker's Steps at Westminster.

The Embankment walls had to be raised and though there were scares towards the end of the nineteenth century the 1881 level was not reached again for nearly half a century. When it happened it was not anticipated. On the night of 6 January 1928 the predicted high water at London Bridge was a safe 12 feet 5 inches and the tide was expected to turn at 1.37 a.m. But a North Sea surge, propelled by strong winds, drove the tide inland where it met a strong flow of fresh water from upriver. The Thames rose alarmingly and at 1 a.m. it stood at 18 feet 3 inches. At Millbank a wall collapsed under the pressure of water and fourteen people were drowned. The calamity could have been far greater as the limits of existing defences had been reached and nobody had been evacuated as the tidal surge was not predicted.

After the 1928 flood the Government called a conference of all London local authorities, the Port of London Authority and the Thames Conservancy Board which then had responsibility for the non-tidal Thames. The flood defences were raised once again, and a research programme instituted which attempted to map and model the forces giving rise to dangerous tides so that they might be predicted. But nothing was done until the aftermath of the great floods which inundated large parts of eastern England and the Thames estuary on the night of 31 January 1953. On Canvey Island fifty-seven people died when the sea defences were breached, unleashing a wall of water which smashed into houses and flooded them instantly. Many people who had been sleeping in upper rooms were rescued as they clung to roofs and, in one case, a picture rail.

*For centuries, the Thames has threatened to overflow its banks and flood London. It has been kept at bay with embankments which have had to be raised regularly since Victorian times. There have been local floods: here a woman is rescued from her home in Clapton, north-east London, when the River Lea which runs into the Thames was swelled with melt-water after the great freeze of 1947.*

London itself was spared in 1953: some of the force of the unpredicted tidal swell was dissipated by the breach in the sea defences downstream. To guard against another exceptional tide the embankment walls would have to be raised again, but it was obvious that in time this would mean that the River Thames would be hidden from view and the problem of sealing the docks in an emergency would become insoluble. A committee was set up by the Government to consider alternative solutions and the distinguished politician appointed to chair it was Lord Waverley, who as Sir John Anderson had been in charge of London's defences during the Blitz and gave his name to the Anderson Shelter.

Waverley's committee reported in 1954 with the suggestion that the only long-term solution to the threat of flooding was some kind of barrier or barrage across the Thames to the east of London which could be shut to hold back a predicted tidal surge. It was not the first time a barrier had been suggested – a system of lock gates was proposed in the 1930s but the problems it would have caused to shipping were considered, on balance, too great. The Thames was London's lifeline as well as a threat to its survival. Disruption to shipping was still a major issue in the 1950s, but when it was calculated that without a barrier river defences would have to be raised six feet above existing levels the argument was effectively over. The questions were: what sort of barrier and where on the Thames should it be built?

It took twenty years to resolve all the technical and adminis-trative problems. In 1968 the scientist and government adviser, Professor Hermann Bondi, reported on a scheme which favoured closing the river off with locks somewhere above Tilbury so that the river upstream of that would no longer be tidal. Professor Bondi thought the gravel reaches of the Thames at low tide were unsightly in London whereas at high tide it was 'one of the great sights of the world, to be put well above Paris and in the same class as Leningrad'. But the ecological effects would have been immense at a time when the river was begin-ning once again to teem with life; there was a danger, too, that the river would silt up without the daily tidal tug of water back to the sea. And in 1968 a large amount of shipping was still coming upriver to the London docks and riverside warehouses which would be held up by the locking system.

The building of the Thames Barrier at Woolwich started in 1974 and it began operations in October 1982. It was first closed against a dangerous tide in February 1983 and officially opened by Her Majesty the Queen in 1984. Downstream, all flood defences had to be raised as a closure of the barrier would naturally increase the river levels there. Rapidly the docks closed down and the amount of shipping passing through the barrier, which remained open most of the time, fell away. London finally had protection against flood disaster. But the barrier was only a temporary measure and will gradually become less and less a guarantee against disaster as the water level of the Thames continues to rise at about eight millimetres a year. A team of the Government's Environmental Agency is already working on new solutions as the barrier is expected to provide protection only until 2030, when rising sea levels as well as the tilting of southeast England will make the present barrier ineffective.

Since it began operation in 1982 the barrier has been closed sixty-seven times against a potential flood. In the winter of 2000 there were twenty-five closures, as the barrier controllers made the complex calculations about exceptional flows of water from upriver in wet weather meeting tidal flows from the coast. It is not just a matter of watching for surges running south from the North Sea. If these hit the Thames estuary when the tide is on the ebb there may not be a problem. But on a flood tide the double action can drive a wall of water upriver. Tides are governed by the phases of the moon and every month there are spring, or high tides, and neap or low tides. A surge coinciding with a spring tide is particularly threatening. But the barrier controllers also have to take into account the flow of fresh water in the Thames, which varies enormously according to the weather inland.

Though Londoners are hardly aware of the fact now, the metropolis is built over many tributaries of the Thames which still flow into the river, though most are hidden below ground and run in drainage pipes. North of the river, from the west there are the River Crane, the Brent, Stamford Brook, the Westbourne, the Tyburn, the Fleet, the Walbrook (in the City) and the River Lea. From the south, again taking the streams from the west, there are Beverley Brook, the River Wandle (which can still be seen as it runs into the Thames west of Wandsworth Bridge), the Falcon, the Effra (in Brixton) and the Ravensbourne. Some of these

*Every year, the water level on the Thames rises: England is tilting east-ward, drawing in the sea, and the embanking of the river has forced the flood tides inland. The greatest flood threat is from a sea-surge rushing in to meet the freshwater river. Since 1982 the capital has been protected by the Thames Barrier at Woolwich which can be opened or closed at short notice. But its life is limited: twenty years from now rising river levels will threaten to overrun it.*

make an appearance as lakes in London parks: the Serpentine in Hyde Park, for example, is fed by the Westbourne, and the lakes in Regent's Park by the Tyburn. One of the tributaries of the Fleet river (after which Fleet Street is named) runs from the ponds on Hampstead Heath.

When there is heavy rain over the London area the surface run-off gathers in these 'lost rivers' and raises the level of the Thames. If an upper river flow rushes down into a rising tide it can produce a flood alert, and the barrier has sometimes been closed to hold back the seaward rush of the river. This is a finely calculated manoeuvre, however, for storm water is often contaminated with pollutants and the longer it is held back the greater the danger to the fish and wildlife of the river.

The continuing and very real threat of a catastrophic flood brings the contemporary significance of the Thames into focus. It is no longer London's commercial lifeline but it has been revived as an ecological resource of national importance. Many species of fish from the North Sea breed in the tidal reaches of the river attracting abundant bird life, especially herons and cormorants. And once again, it has become a favoured strand on which to build homes. There are plans to extend the present dockland developments to the east, both north and south of the river, so that tens of thousands more Londoners will live within the Thames flood plain. It seems that the river is regaining some of the character it had in the mid-eighteenth century, with row upon row of housing overlooking the river and commuters whisked into central London on a river bus. But all these plans will have to be abandoned if a long-term solution to the flood danger is not found.

It is too early to say what strategy will be favoured to hold back the Thames tides in the mid-twenty-first century, but a plan which would allow the river to return to its more natural state is being given very serious consideration. London was saved from catastrophe in 1953 in part because the flood waters spread over large areas of the estuary. In Kent and Essex the consequences were tragic. However, it might be possible to allow for an incoming tide to wash over large areas of uninhabited land on either bank of the estuary such as the old salt marshes. One reason the tides push so far inland is that the river has over many centuries been hemmed in: if it were released well below London there might be no need for a new barrier and higher flood defences. But there is time yet to enjoy the riverside in London: the odds against a serious flood before 2030 are around 2000 to 1.

# Bibliography

Hilaire Belloc, *The Historic Thames*, illustrations by A.R. Quinton, introductions by Alan C. Jenkins (Exeter: Webb & Bower, 1988)

Richard Burnell, *One Hundred and Fifty Years of the Oxford and Cambridge Boat Race: an Official History* (Marlow: Precision Press, 1979)

Charles Dickens (Jr), *Dickens's Dictionary of the Thames, from its Source to the Nore* (1890; reprinted Taurus Press, 1972)

Frank L. Dix, *Royal River Highway: a History of the Passenger Boats and Services on the River Thames* (Newton Abbot: David & Charles, 1985)

John Doxat, *The Living Thames: the Restoration of a Great Tidal River* (Hutchinson, 1977)

Chris Ellmers and Alex Werner, *London's Riverscape, Lost and Found: a Photographic Panorama* (Viking, 1988)

Chris Ellmers and Alex Werner, *Dockland Life: a Pictorial History of London's Docks 1860–2000* (Edinburgh: Mainstream, 2000)

Henry Humpherus, *History of the Origin and Progress of the Company of Watermen and Lightermen of the River Thames, with numerous historical notes, 1514–1859* (reprinted E.P. Microform Ltd, 1981)

Bill Luckin, *Pollution and Control: a Social History of the Thames in the Nineteenth Century* (Hilger, 1986)

Henry Mayhew, *London Labour and the London Poor*, introduction by John D. Rosenberg (1849; Constable, 1968)

Geoffrey Phillips, *Thames Crossings, Bridges, Tunnels and Ferries* (Newton Abbot: David & Charles, 1981)

Gavin Weightman, *London River: the Thames Story* (Collins & Brown, 1990)

Alwyne Wheeler, *The Tidal Thames: the History of a River and its Fishes* (Routledge & Kegan Paul, 1979)

# Picture Credits

The author and publishers would like to thank the following for permission to reproduce illustrations: pp. 3 and 135, Hulton Archive; p. 7, Museum of London; pp. 12, 13, 14, 16, 19, 22, 24, 26, 30, 42, 44, 53, 61, 70, 77, 81, 97, 115, 121 and 122, Guildhall Library, Corporation of London; pp. 88 and 129, Mary Evans Picture Library; p. 108, Wingfield Sporting Gallery, London/Bridgeman Art Library, London; p. 112, Science Museum/Science & Society Picture Library; p. 138, Adam Woolfitt/CORBIS.

# Index

Page numbers in *italic* indicate illustrations